BOOK

OF

THE LODGE,

OR

OFFICER'S MANUAL.

BY

THE REV. G. OLIVER, D. D.,

AUTHOR OF

"THE HISTORICAL LANDMARKS," "THE HISTORY OF INITIATION," "ANTIQUITIES OF FREEMASONRY," "STAR IN THE EAST," ETC. ETC. ETC.

PAST D. G. M. OF THE GRAND LODGE OF MASSACHUSETTS, U. S. PAST D. P. G. M. FOR LINCOLNSHIRE.

HONORARY MEMBER OF THE BANK OF ENGLAND LODGE, LONDON; THE SHAKSPEARE LODGE, WARWICK; THE FIRST LODGE OF LIGHT, BIRMINGHAM; THE ST. PETER'S LODGE, WOLVERHAMPTON; THE WITHAM LODGE, LINCOLN; THE ST. PETER'S LODGE, PETERBOROUGH; LIGHT OF THE NORTH LODGE, LONDONDERRY; ROYAL STANDARD LODGE, KIDDERMINSTER; LODGE RISING STAR WESTERN INDIA, BOMBAY; ST. GEORGE'S LODGE, MONTREAL; LODGE, SOCIAL FRIENDSHIP, MADRAS; ETC.

Αθηνων των Θεοδμητων.—SOPHOCLES.

Gaecos Teletas ac Mysteria taciturnitate parietibusque clausisse.
VARRO.

Cornerstone Book Publishers
New Orleans, LA
2016 Photographic Reproduction

1849.

The Book of the Lodge
by George Oliver
Foreword by Michael R. Poll

A Cornerstone Book
Published by Cornerstone Book Publishers
Copyright © 2016 & 2020 by Cornerstone Book Publishers

Cornerstone Book Publishers
New Orleans, LA

First Cornerstone Edition – 2016
Second Cornerstone Edition - 2020

www.cornerstonepublishers.com

ISBN- 9781613423493

MADE IN THE USA

Foreword to the Cornerstone Edition

When I joined Freemasonry, I was deeply moved by the philosophy and moral lessons that were taught in the ritual and monitors. I believe that what moved me the most was that so many of the teachings were layered. By that I mean, the lessons were presented in a way that if you wished to only consider the outer teachings, that was fine. But, if you wanted to dig deeper, there was so much more to discover. For me, this was the true beauty of Freemasonry. You could custom tailor the teachings for everyone. You could go as far as your ability and interest took you.

Let's look at just one aspect of our operation and things we say in lodge. In the lodge, we say that we all "meet upon the level." The clear message being sent is that we are all equal. All the members of the lodge are on the same "level." That sounds nice, but it's hardly true.

Some years back, I revised the classic *Robert's Rules of Order* into a Masonic edition. As was pointed out in the revised edition, the office of Worshipful Master has far greater authority, rights, and power than the presiding officers of clubs. It's one of the reasons why the classic, unrevised edition of *Roberts Rules of Order* is so problematic for a Masonic lodge. The membership of a lodge is simply not equal in authority to the Worshipful Master.

In fact, in society we are not all equal. We most certainly have equal value as human beings, but we all have different abilities, skills, and levels of knowledge. One person may be good at singing, another at building things, or art, or science, or on and on. We all have some things that we are good at and some things at which we are not so good. If we were all equal, we would be photocopies, or clones, of each other. That's not the case. We are all individually distinct human beings.

So, what do we mean when we say that we are all "upon the level"? If you stop and think about our degrees, teachings, and rituals, you will see that we provide the same rituals and teachings to all our candidates. Yes, each jurisdiction is a little different and the rituals vary a little to a great deal. But the basic elements of initiation and the story line are the same no matter the ritual, rite, or jurisdiction. We all teach the Hiramic Legend. Maybe it is a little different from jurisdiction to jurisdiction, but the basic elements are the same.

All candidates and initiates are given the same basic symbolic tools and opportunities. All candidates are given the same message through the degrees: "Here are symbolic working tools that you can, if you choose, make use of to create improvements in yourself." The choice of taking advantage of the teachings and lessons is always 100% up to the initiates. No one is going to force anyone to grow, advance or be anything that they do not choose to be.

When we say that we are all on the level, it doesn't mean that we all have the same skills, talents, strengths, or weaknesses. It also does not mean that everyone avails themselves at the same level or chooses to participate in all the teachings.

In the days of the old Operative Freemasons, they used the level as an actual working tool for their profession. It was used to assure their work was quality work. The old Operatives earned their livings by the value of the work that they did. Proper use of their tools assured them that they would continue to work.

In Speculative Freemasonry it's not required that we take advantage of the symbolic lessons that we are given. We will not be fired from our Masonry if we do not grow because of the lessons that we are given. We can just sit back in lodge and enjoy the show.

While sitting back, failing to grow, and basically doing nothing but being there would have resulted in an Operative Mason being thrown out of the lodge, the same is not true with us. In fact, just sitting there, or being there, in some lodges can result in your election to become a lodge leader. That's the *real* problem with some lodges. We are simply not all equal in ability, skill, and performance. If the only ability that the lodge needs for its leadership positions is the ability to show up, then the lodge is in far more danger than it realizes.

The symbol of the level teaches that we all have the same value as human beings. It doesn't matter as to our skill set, any abilities that we may, or may not have, or the level of our personal growth because of the lessons we are given. As a human being, we are all due equal respect, fair treatment, and basic decency. But the lodge is also due the very same things. We must be fair and respectful to the lodge as well as the members. If one member is particularly good at ritual and your close friend is horrible at ritual, do you pick your friend as the lodge ritualist because we are all on the level?

Being on the level means only that we are all given the same lessons and opportunity to learn and grow. We are all valued, respected, and treated the same. Being on the level does not mean that we are all assumed to instantly possess the same abilities, skills, or experiences. Being fair does not mean that we get what we want simply because we want it.

And this brings us to George Oliver's *The Book of the Lodge*. I'm not going to represent that this is the only book that a Mason will need. I will, however, tell you that this is a valuable book for the new or experienced Mason. This book will provide insight and answers to Masons seeking greater knowledge into Freemasonry and its meaning. From general information of the Masonic Order to the structure of the lodge and duties of officers, this is a book of value. This book can help educate any Mason to the level that they seek education.

The lessons of Freemasonry require study and often restudy. We grow in Masonry because of the work we put into our study. The best lesson that we can take away from this aspect of Masonic philosophy is that we need to be dead honest with ourselves about ourselves. We are not to allow that little green devil known as envy to force us to focus on others who may have different, or greater, talents in certain areas than us. We *all* have our own unique talents — discovered or undiscovered. We are to focus on ourselves and the work that we need to do to reach our own full potential. We are in competition with only ourselves. Through the study of Masonic literature, we can discover unrealized depths of both Freemasonry and us.

Enjoy *The Book of the Lodge*. Allow it to open doors for you and deepen your appreciation of our Fraternity. Cornerstone is proud to offer this enlightened work for your consideration.

Fraternally,
Michael R. Poll
Cornerstone Book Publishers

The Author's Address

TO THE

FRATERNITY.

MY DEAR BRETHREN,

It is well known that throughout my whole life I have been, not merely a lover of Masonry, but an enthusiast—a champion for the purity of its forms and ceremonies—zealous for its uninterrupted prosperity—and fearful lest the world should misunderstand its references, or misinterpret its benevolent designs. Sensitively alive to its interests and reputation, I have defended it with my utmost abilities, and have mourned when the misconduct of an individual brother, has given its enemies an advantage, and caused them to exult in an

PREFACE.

early masonic days, before I became acquainted
with the true bearing and excellence of the
institution, the bitter mortification to which I
found myself subjected, when an expert an-
tagonist advanced arguments against the Order,
which I was not prepared to refute; for the
masonic literature of that day was circumscribed within a very narrow compass, and
extended information on the subject of masonry was difficult of attainment.

It is a matter of infinite gratification to me,
that this unfavourable state of things no longer
exists, and that I have lived to a period when
the fraternity have roused themselves to a
sense of duty, and entertain a feeling that the
dignity of Freemasonry requires some exertions
on their part, to promote its popularity, and
place it on a level with other scientific institutions; and who for this great purpose, employ
their talents through the medium of the Press,
to display its utility as a benevolent Order,
promoting at once the investigations of science,
and the practice of every moral and social virtue.

PREFACE.

For several years I have been in the habit of receiving letters from brethren in different parts of the kingdom, who have been entrusted with the arrangement of any important masonic celebration, enquiring into the usages of antiquity on particular points, that the ceremonial may be conducted in strict accordance with the Constitutions of the Order. A marked anxiety so uniformly displayed amongst the whole body of masons, has suggested the propriety of some general answers to all enquiries of this nature, as a measure which would not only be well received, but hailed as a boon by the fraternity at large.

For this purpose it is not to be doubted but that a Manual embracing legitimate information on all cases which can possibly arise, will be peculiarly acceptable to the W. Masters and Officers of a Lodge in particular, and to every brother who is desirous of becoming well versed in the usages and customs of masonry in primitive times.

On this plan, therefore, the present little volume has been constructed. The information which it contains has been carefully arranged by a comparison of the rites practised by our ancient brethren, with those which are enjoined by the United Grand Lodge of England; and it appears extremely probable that the fraternity would glady adopt an uniformity of practice on points where they have hitherto been at a loss to determine whether ceremonies of constant recurrence are, or are not, in accordance with ancient usage.

In this enquiry the customs of foreign Lodges have not been overlooked; and it is hoped that this little volume will constitute an unerring book of reference which cannot fail to be of incalculable service to the fraternity. It is almost entirely practical; and the directions have been drawn up in strict conformity with the Constitutions of our own Grand Lodge; so that the brethren may adopt them in full confidence that they are as sound and legitimate as if they had been enjoined by authority.

G. O.

Scopwick Vicarage,
January 1st, 1849.

CONTENTS.

THE AUTHOR'S ADDRESS TO THE FRATERNITY.

CHAP. I. WHAT IS MASONRY? Its nature and influence—Symbolical Masonry defined—Arts taught by Freemasonry—its high antiquity—morality of the order—Know thyself—universality of Masonry—its benevolent character—in whom do you put your trust?—tongue of good report—open to all—symbolical—ancient charges—tendency of the Lectures—symbol of a Lodge—equality—secrets of Masonry incommunicable.

CHAP. II. THE LODGE. Initiation of a candidate—definitions—what is a Lodge?—a microcosm—extent—ground—pavement—star—border—covering—Pedestal—Lights, &c. all minutely explained.

CHAP. III. THE RITUAL OF BUILDING. Why a mason's Lodge differs from an ordinary building—utility of ceremonies—exhibited to the dead—preparations for building—the ritual—the plan—proper situation of a masonic hall—position of the windows—altitude—roof—approaches—entrances—screens—chapels or closets—various other particulars.

CHAP. IV. THE FOUNDATION STONE. The appropriate time of levelling the footstone of a masonic hall—number of brethren necessary to begin the work—notices—duty of P. G. Masters and masters of lodges—preliminary arrangements—instructions for ceremonial—assembly of brethren—full and copious detail of all the rites and ceremonies of laying the foundation stone.

CONTENTS.

CHAP. V. THE DECORATIONS. Furniture of a lodge—of the walls—embellishments—curtains—dais—screen—pedestal—appropriate passages of scripture for opening the Holy Bible in the several degrees—ornaments—transparencies—candlesticks—statues or paintings—carpet—general harmony of design.

CHAP. VI. THE NAME. Improper names—importance of—due consideration necessary—names ought to be appropriate—precedency—the Number of a lodge—why lodges are named—its utility—superstitions attached to names—ancient mysteries and miracle plays—moralities—Names derived from—the period when names of Lodges were first imposed.

CHAP. VII. THE CONSECRATION. Necessity of dedication and consecration—duty of director of ceremonies—processions—preliminary arrangements—instructions to the brethren—Ceremony of Consecration minutely described—duties of Masters—order of procession—religious services at the Church—sermon—return to the lodge room.

CHAP. VIII. THE PILLAR OF WISDOM. Union of the fraternity—form of government—laws—constitutions—landmarks—rulers of a lodge—power of a Master—his duties—his qualifications—and tact—impropriety of electing inadequate Masters—evil consequences of—degree of Past Master—description of a good W. M.—how to govern a lodge profitably—the Bye-Laws—regularity and decorum—admission of candidates—improper persons to be rejected—results of good government—peace, harmony, and brotherly-love.

CHAP. IX. THE PILLARS OF STRENGTH AND BEAUTY. Duty of the Wardens—Jewel of the S. W.—his place in the lodge—regularity of attendance recommended—Jewel of the J. W.—his place and duties—the Deacons—the office unknown till a recent period—the officer of the South, who?—E. A. P.'s originally had a vote in Grand Lodge—enquiry into the first appointment of Deacons—their Jewel—continental officers of a lodge—duties of the members of a lodge—mutual obligations—happy results.

CONTENTS.

CHAP. X. TRACING BOARD OF AN E. A. P. Bro. Harris's new Tracing Boards considered—progress of a candidate through the degrees—instruction—the ground, situation, extent, support, and covering of a lodge, explained in detail —east and west—three Pillars—mosaic work—jewels—symbols—working tools—ashlars—lewis—the Holy Bible—pedestal—great lights—ladder—blazing star.

CHAP. XI. TRACING BOARD OF A F. C., AND A M. M. The new Fellowcraft's tracing boards noticed—Jeptha and the Ephraimites—the river Jordon—winding staircase—working tools—the two Pillars—view of the Holy Place—queen of Sheba—decorations—lights—altar of incense—Sanctum Sanctorum—the veils—Tracing Board of the Third Degree —emblems of mortality—the veil withdrawn—ark—Mercy Seat—cherubims—Shekinah—the centre—working tools—ornaments—custom of decking graves with flowers—uncertainty of life—resurrection of the dead—the way to die happily.

CHAP. XII. LABOUR AND REFRESHMENT. Arrangement of the lodge furniture in the last century—the primitive floor cloth—masonic labor—explanations—refreshment—its propriety—disuse of during lodge hours—duty of the J. W.—approval of moderate refreshment—toasts and songs—social intercourse—libels on masonic refreshment—moderation of the fraternity—temperance and total abstinence considered.

THE BOOK OF THE LODGE.

CHAP. I.

WHAT IS MASONRY?

" King Athelstan caused a general assembly of all masons in the realme at York, and there made many masons, and gave them a deepe charge for observation of such articles as belong to masonry, and delivered them a charter to keepe, and when his Assembly was gathered together he caused a cry to be made, that if any mason of them had a writing that did concerne masonry, or could informe the King in anything or matter that wanting in the said Science already delivered, that they or hee should deliver them to the King or write them to him: and there were some in French, some in Greeke, some in English, and other languages ; whereupon the King caused a Book to be made, which declared how the Science was first invented, and the utility thereof; which Book he commanded to be read and plainly declared when a man was to be made a mason, that he might fully understand what Articles, Rules, and Orders, he was obliged to observe ; and from that time untill this day Masonry hath been much respected and preserved ; and divers new Articles hath been added to the sayd charge, by good advise and consent of the best Masons and Fellowes."—ANCIENT MASONIC MANUSCRIPT.

THE tendency of Freemasonry is sometimes mistaken, not only by the uninitiated, but also by many of those who have been superficially instructed in its mysteries. One considers it to be an institution framed for the purposes of benevolence ; that, through its medium, the sick may be visited, the destitute relieved, the widow

B

comforted, and the aged placed in a situation where want can never more afflict them. But this design, how amiable and praiseworthy soever it may be, is only one of the purposes of Freemasonry; and if, as this class of brethren suppose, it were confined to these charitable ends, it would rank merely on a level with a common Friendly Society, or Sick Club. Others suppose it to be connected with artisans and operative stonemasons; judging from the instruments of mechanical craft which form the chief symbols of the order, that this must be its principal reference;—while some take it for a mere convivial society, whose exclusiveness in the selection of its members is guarded by signs and tokens, the payment of a heavy fine at admission, and the adoption of a peculiar dress.

There are other opinions afloat, even amongst the brethren themselves; some of whom frequently display such a frigid indifference to the peculiarity of its construction, and are so insensible to the great and apparent advantages which result from its complicated organization, embracing history and legend, science and morals, and blending the practice of virtue with the enjoyment of moderate conviviality,—as to afford a reasonable pretext to those who are uninitiated for taking no interest in the institution, and for repressing any desire which they might otherwise have entertained to " ask that they might have, to seek that they might find, and to knock that the door of masonry might be opened to them."

Symbolical masonry, under whatever form it may be propounded, is a catholic institution, democratic in its form and government, and universal in its operation. This is demonstrable from any of the definitions of the order;—from the free election of its chief magistrate and the inferior governors of every private lodge, annually and by universal suffrage;—and from the reputed form, and symbolical extent of its lodges. If it were deprived of any of the above attributes, it would be no longer Freemasonry; and all its beneficial effects upon the mind and manners of men, would be scattered to the winds of heaven. That this conclusion is not unwarranted, we will proceed to test it by an enquiry into the nature of the institution, and its peculiarity of construction; which will clearly prove its universality, and the free application of its principles to every inhabitant of the globe who acknowledges the Being of a God, whatever be his colour, religion, education, or mental qualifications.

A consideration of the definitions of Freemasonry which have been given in different ages, and by different writers, will clear the way, and form a preliminary step to the consideration of its general principles, and show in what manner they are applicable to all mankind in every age and nation.

1. In a MS. which has the reputation of having been written by King Henry VI., we have this definition of masonry. " Ytt beeth the skylle of nature, the understondynge of the myghte that

ys hereyune, and its sondrye werkynges; sonder-
lyche, the skylle of reckenyngs, of waightes and
metynges, and the true manere of façonnynge al
thynges for mannes use; headlye, dwellinges, and
buyldynges of alle kindes, and all other thynges
that make gudde to manne." And again, the same
document asserts that the arts which have been
taught to mankind by masons, are "agricultura,
architectura, astronomia, geometria, numeres, mu-
sica, poesie, kymistrye, governmente, and relygy-
onne."

In these definitions we find nothing of an exclusive or unapproachable nature ; for natural,
mathematical, and mechanical knowledge, have
been practised in every age, and by every people
upon the face of the globe. Whether we turn
our eyes to the east or to the west—to India
and China—Egypt and Greece—Scandinavia and
Britain—Mexico and Peru—the remote islands of
Australia on the one hand, or Iceland and Spitz-
bergen on the other—we shall find every where
traces of genius and skill of the highest antiquity,
which excite our astonishment, and prove beyond
a doubt, that how proud soever we may be of our
progress in the above arts and sciences, we were
equalled, and in some instances surpassed, by those
primitive nations. The monuments of India and
Egypt, with those of what we denominate the
New World, exhibit the perfection of science, and
the triumphs of human ingenuity ; as the ruins of
Herculaneum and Pompeii have thrown open to

our inspection the elegance and luxury of the
Greeks and Romans at the period when these
cities were destroyed by the fearful eruptions of
Mount Vesuvius in the time of Titus, a short time
after the destruction of the temple of Jerusalem.

Recent discoveries in central America have
made us acquainted with a series of facts which
display the scientific acquirements of an unknown people, whose antiquity cannot even be
conjectured. Stephens, in his "Incidents of
Travel," has the following reflections in the midst
of the magnificent ruins of Copan in Mexico.
"There were no associations connected with the
place; none of those stirring recollections which
hallow Rome, Athens, and the world's great mis-
tress on the Egyptian plain; but architecture,
sculpture, and painting, all the arts which embel-
lish life, had flourished in this overgrown forest;
orators, warriors, and statesmen; beauty, ambition,
and glory, had lived and passed away, and none
knew that such things had been, or could tell of
their past existence. Books, the records of knowledge, are silent on this theme. The city is deso-
late. No remnant of this race hangs round the
ruins, with traditions handed down from father to
son, and from generation to generation. It lay
before us like a shattered bark in the midst of the
ocean ; her masts gone, her name effaced, her crew
perished, and none to tell whence she came, to
whom she belonged, how long on her voyage, or
what caused her destruction ; her lost people to be

B 5

traced only by some fancied resemblance in the construction of the vessel, and perhaps never to be known at all. The place where we sat—was it a citadel, from which an unknown people had sounded the trumpet of war? or a temple for the worship of the god of peace? or did the inhabitants worship the idols made with their own hands, and offer sacrifices on the stones before them? All was mystery; dark, impenetrable mystery; and every circumstance increased it. In Egypt the colossal skeletons of gigantic temples stand in the unwatered sands in all the nakedness of desolation;—here an immense forest shrouds the ruins, hiding them from sight, heightening the impression and moral effect, and giving an intensity and almost wildness to the interest." One thing however is quite certain. These ruins exhibit a knowledge of the sciences, which is not surpassed by any nation of the ancient world.

The arts then being of universal application— Freemasonry—which teaches those arts, is of universal application also; and hence cosmopolitical.

2. The next definition of masonry which I shall adduce in proof of the same proposition, was propounded at the revival of masonry by Dr. Anderson, the learned author of the History and Constitutions of Masonry, whose opinion, in those days was considered decisive on every point connected with the order. As the former related exclusively to science, this is confined to morals; and will be found equally comprehensive.   "The end, the

moral, and purport of masonry is, to subdue our passions, not to do our own will; to make a daily progress in a laudable art, and to promote morality, charity, good fellowship, good nature, and humanity." [1]

I have considered this definition with great attention, and cannot find anything exclusive in the terms by which it is set forth. It is applicable to all mankind, in every situation, condition, and religion. There can be no exceptions to the universality of its principles; and the virtues which it enjoins, may be practised by old and young of both sexes, in all nations, whether savage or civilized. To subdue the passions has been the universal aim of mankind. All have placed their hopes upon it; and hence sprang the first idea of the Γνῶθι σεαυτον, which was inscribed on the portal of the heathen temples, that it might prove a stimulus to virtue, of which it was the first lesson, and lead to the desirable consummation in which all excellence was blended, of subduing the passions. Few attained this blessed serenity of mind, but Socrates was amongst the number; for Zopyrus, an eminent physiognomist, having declared that he discovered in the features of that philosopher evident traces of many vicious passions; the friends of Socrates derided his judgment, which they declared was eminently at variance with fact. But Socrates acknowledged his penetration; confessing that he was naturally dispo-

1 Golden Remains, Vol. 1. p. 49.

sed to vicious indulgences, but that he had subdued his passions by reason and philosophy.

Amongst the early Christians, many of whose names have been inscribed on the lists of the order, whether truly or not is immaterial to our present purpose, this result was frequently acquired; of which the history of the persecutions affords numerous instances; and without it the religion of Christ could not have been successfully promulgated in the midst of dangers, and under the constant dread of bonds, imprisonment, and death. Tacitus thus mentions the facts. "Their sufferings at their execution were aggravated by insult and mockery; for some were disguised in the skins of wild beasts, and worried to death by dogs; some were crucified; and others were wrapped in pitch shirts, and set on fire when the day closed, that they might serve as lights to illuminate the night." And Juvenal, to the same purport says "they were subjected to be burned in their own flame and smoke, their head being held up by a stake fixed to their chin, till they made a long stream of blood and melted sulphur on the ground." And they endured these accumulated sufferings with a constancy that elicited the admiration even of their enemies. They had a great contempt for the things of this world, and cherished such strong hopes of immortality, that they surrendered themselves cheerfully to sufferings, and despised death under whatever fearful form it might be presented to them.

Here then we have a clear proof that the early christians practised the moral definition masonry. They subdued their passions; did not their own will; made a daily progress in a laudable art; and practised morality, charity, goodnature, and humanity.

If we turn to the savages of the east or the west, we shall find the same general principle exemplified;—they attained such a mastery over their passions under circumstances the most distressing, that when the fortune of war placed them in the hands of their enemies, they despised torment and courted death; and instead of trying to conciliate their persecutors, they taunted them with their own performances, and dared them to proceed to the utmost extremity of inflicting pain; dying at length with a song in their mouth, and joy and peacefulness in their hearts.

So extensive was the operation of masonic principles, even in the absence of masonry itself; and so boundless was the influence of those peculiar virtues which it recommends and enforces, that their operation may justly be pronounced to be universal in extent, and consequently unlimited in its practice.

3. The next definition we meet with was promulgated about the middle of the 18th century. It is peculiarly cosmopolitical, and requires no explanation to point out its universal tendency. "Masonry is a science confined to no particular country, but extends over the whole terrestrial

globe. Wherever arts flourish, there it flourishes also. Add to this, that by secret and inviolable signs, carefully preserved among the fraternity, it becomes an universal language. Hence many advantages are gained ;—the distant Chinese, the wild Arab, and the American savage, will embrace a brother Briton, and know, that besides the common ties of humanity, there is still a stronger obligation to induce him to kind and friendly offices."

4. " Freemasonry is a benevolent order, instituted by virtuous men, for the praiseworthy purpose of spreading the blessings of morality and science amongst all ranks and descriptions of men."

5. " Freemasonry is the grand and universal science which includes all others, but having a more immediate reference to those branches which teach us a knowledge of ourselves, and our duty to others."

These definitions of masonry convey the same truth, that its purposes are benevolent, and being spread over the whole universe, operate, without respect of persons to make men happy in this world, with the hope of having it increased in the world to come. Like the former definitions, they refer, not only to the inhabitants living in the 19th century, wheresoever dispersed under the wide and lofty canopy of heaven, but to all nations, kindreds, and people, from the formation of the world. In this respect it is like christianity, which is also a cosmopolite institution, comprehending all mankind in one fold under one shepherd, and embracing them in the universal scheme of unlimited redemption. There never was any nation under heaven, how savage soever its inhabitants might be, who had not some notion of a Supreme Being, and a future state of existence. Their opinions were often fanciful, and frequently erroneous, but none were buried in a gloomy atheism. Each had its scale of virtue which was reputed to translate them to the Good Spirit after death.

Amongst the principal nations of the earth, a peculiar institution was in existence which promised eternal happiness in Elysium to all who were initiated into its mysteries; while the deepest and most painful carverns of Tartarus were allotted to the atheist, and the despiser of these celebrations. Thus Cicero asserts that it is by the influence of the Mysteries that mankind are drawn from a savage life, and modelled by humanity. Hence they are called *Initia*, because they are the beginings of a life of reason and virtue; and men receive from them a superior degree of happiness here, with the promise of a better life hereafter. And Plato says to the same effect. " In my opinion the institutors of the Mysteries were well acquainted with the manners and dispositions of men; for in these rites the aspirants were taught that those who died without being initiated, would for ever stick fast in the mud and filth of Tartarus; while those who were purified by initiation, should, after death, be advanced to the habitations of the celestial deities."

In these extracts we find principles enunciated which correspond in a great measure with the above definitions of Freemasonry; and show that similar ideas existed, and produced the same conclusions in every age and nation of the world; for the precepts of our noble order have been admitted throughout all time, as the best calculated to produce human happiness here, and lead to a more perfected and ineffable bliss hereafter. The patriarchs practised it, and founded their dearest hopes upon it. The Jews professed it, although they did not in practice conform to its dictates, as may be instanced in the case of the woman taken in adultery. "Her crime was manifest," says Dean Kirwan, "and her punishment exactly laid down in the law; yet it filled the just soul of the Redeemer with indignation, to see men so criminal as the Pharasees, the slaves of every passion, under the mask of extraordinary zeal, standing forward with clamour and eagerness, to avenge the violated law; he therefore answered them in a way not to palliate the offence, but which strikingly conveyed the indispensable concomitant of true zeal,—Let the man who is without sin amongst you cast the first stone at this unfortunate woman!" A decision too pointed not to have a most apt and a most humiliating effect; for, as the Evangelist reports, "they retired one after another silent and confounded."

Even the heathen eulogised the beauty of virtue, although they misapplied the term, and believed it to consist in practices which revelation condemns in the strongest terms. " Disciplines," says Hippodamus the Pythagorean, " are the sources of erudition, and cause the desires to be impelled to virtue. But the laws, partly detaining by fear, repel men from the commission of crimes, and partly alluring by honours and gifts, excite them to virtue. And manners and studies fashion the soul like wax, and through their continued energy impress in it propensities that become, as it were, natural. It is necessary, however, that these three should have an arrangement in conjunction with the beautiful, the useful, and the just; and that each of these three should, if possible, have all these for its final intention; but if not all of them, it should at least have two or one of them as the mark at which it aims, in order that *disciplines, manners,* and *laws,* may be beautiful, just, and advantageous."

This reasoning is purely masonic; but if we refer to the lives of those to whom this man preached, we shall find them replete with conduct which is in direct opposition to the precepts, because they mistook the meaning of the word virtue, and classed on an equality with it, many unsocial, selfish, and fiend-like passions. How different are the conclusions of our glorious science, which centre all the benevolent affections of the mind in charity and Brotherly Love. In the words of one who was not a mason by initiation, but was truly a brother in his heart, "how perfective of human nature and human happiness that system is, which, even in the face of an enemy, observes a brother; which is one continued line of exhortation to unbounded benevolence, and whose illustrious founder has declared, that its professors should be known and immortalized by that one sentiment alone ; thus pointing out the means of beginning our heaven upon earth, and antedating here below the joys and tranquillity of the blessed."

6. "Speculative masonry is so far interwoven with religion, as to lay us under the strongest obligations to pay that rational homage to the deity, which at once constitutes our duty and our happiness. It leads the contemplative to view with reverence and admiration the glorious works of creation and inspires them with the most exalted ideas of the perfections of the Divine Creator."

Here we have a direct assertion of the universality of masonry, for the precept is applicable to all people that ever existed, or that ever shall exist throughout the whole course of time. The homage which is due from the creature to the Creator is a natural feeling, implanted in the heart by the deity himself, and existing with the most barbarous as well as the most enlightened people. None, who saw the course of the sun by day, the moon and the stars by night, the growth of vegetables, summer and winter, seedtime and harvest, could

be ignorant of the existence of some superintend-
ing phenomena;—every thing preserving the most
perfect order and regularity; for the most barbarous and savage people—possessing but a single
spark of reason—could not be induced to believe
that the sun and the moon occupied their places
by chance, that by the effect of accident the trees
put out their buds at one season of the year, the
blossoms and leaves at another, which ripened into
fruit in a third, and were cast aside in a fourth,
because they were useless in an inclement winter.
Even Aristotle, who, if not an absolute atheist,
was on the very verge of it, could say, "that to
believe the gods to be the first beings, is a divine
truth; and that, though arts and sciences have
probably been often lost and revived, yet this opinion has been preserved as a relic to this very time."

There is an excellent passage to the same effect
in a writer of the last century, which is worth
preserving. "The judgment that every wicked
man necessarily and immediately makes concerning any unjust act of another, by which he himself
happens to suffer, will for ever convict him of
knowing well that difference of moral good and
evil, which he is not willing to acknowledge, or
which he is not willing to make the rule of his
own behaviour. This is what the Apostle calls
the law written in men's hearts, by which they
are a law unto themselves, their conscience also
bearing witness, and their thoughts the meanwhile
accusing or excusing one another; therefore it is

certain men are naturally conscious of the difference of good and evil, and of the consequent desert of their own actions. It is natural for them to apprehend that this judgment of their own consciences is the judgment that God also passes upon them; and the scripture very clearly affirms that it is so."

From such arguments we deduce the universal application of the definitions of masonry under our present notice, in proof of the fact that the order is cosmopolitical.

7. " The zeal of masons in the acquisition of knowledge is bounded by no space, since they travel from east to west in its pursuit; and the principles which actuate them are highly conducive to morality; viz., the attempt to rule and govern the passions, and to keep a tongue of good report, that where candour cannot commend, silence will, at least, avoid reproach."

8. " The masonic system exhibits a stupendous and beautiful fabric, founded on universal piety, unfolding its gates to receive, without prejudice or discrimination, the worthy professors of every description of genuine religion ; concentrating, as it were, into one body, their just tenets, unincumbered by the disputable peculiarities of all sects and persuasions."

These definitions need no comment. The reference which they contain to universality, to the application of masonry by all religious sects, and the professors of every mode of faith who practice genuine religion in its purity, are too evident to be denied, and too plain to admit of dubitation or dispute. They exhibit a beautiful picture of the genius of masonry opening wide her arms of benevolence to receive the children of men; like the Saviour of mankind inviting his creatures to accept the salvation which he freely offers without money and without price. " Come unto me all ye that labour and are heavy laden, and I will give you rest. Take my yoke upon you, and learn of me; for I am meek and lowly in heart; and you shall find rest unto your souls. For my yoke is easy, and my burden is light."[2] And his benevolent intentions are confirmed by St. Paul in his cosmopolite assertion that " there is neither Jew nor Greek, there is neither bond nor free, there is neither male nor female; for ye are all one in Christ Jesus."[3] And again, with more universality of application in another place, " there is neither Greek nor Jew, circumcision nor uncircumcision, Barbarian, Scythian, bond nor free; but Christ is all and in all."[4]

9. " Masonry is a beautiful system of morality, veiled in allegory, and illustrated by symbols."

This illustration, when divested of its first member, is peculiarly applicable to all those remarkable institutions which prevailed amongst heathen nations, and were denominated Mysteries, but are now called the Spurious Freemasonry.

[2] Mat. xi. 28, to end. [3] Gal. iii. 28.
[4] Col. iii. 11.

It is true, they eulogised morality in pompous language, but practised it not; or more correctly speaking, understood it not. Ovid affirms,

Ingenuas didicisse fideliter artes,
Emollit mores, nec sinit esse feros ;

a sentiment which is extremely apposite, and embodies an attribute of masonry; for by the study of the sciences, our order asserts that we acquire a propensity to benevolence, and a desire to be useful to our fellow creatures. Horace, however, excludes morality from the practice of his " good man," and confines it to obedience to the laws of our country. Vir bonus est quis ! Qui consulta patrum, qui leges juraque servat.

Charondas, the Catanæan philosopher, thus recommends morality. " Wanton insolence and injustice are the attendants of shamelessness and impudence. And destruction follows these. Let, however, no one be impudent, but let every one be modest and temperate; because he will thus have the gods propitious to him, and will procure for himself salvation. For no vicious man is dear to divinity. Let every one likewise honour probity and truth, and hate what is base and false ; for these are the indications of virtue and vice."

It will be unnecessary to multiply instances of the love of virtue amongst the heathen in theory —the fact is notorious. But the fate of their best and most virtuous men will show the kind of estimation in which their moral harangues were held

by the people. Pythagoras was slain. As he sat
in council with his friends in the house of Milo, it
was set on fire by some one out of envy because
he had been refused admission. Pythagoras made
his escape, for the envious man had vowed to take
away his life; and having procured the assistance
of a few unworthy men the philosopher was hotly
pursued. Coming to a place full of beans, he
stopped short saying, "it is better to be taken
than to tread amongst the beans; it is better to
be killed than to speak," and his pursuers accordingly slew him. In a similar manner most of his
disciples lost their lives. Aristides was banished
from his country out of envy, because by his upright and virtuous conduct he had acquired the
appellation of "the Just." Alcibiades was killed
by a faction; Socrates was put to death for his
virtues; and it was at all times dangerous for any
one to be celebrated for his benevolence, justice,
or kindness to the poor.

If we take a view of the heathen morality
through the medium of its public institutions, we
shall not enjoy a more favourable picture of its
operation. Law and religion were equally sangui-
nary; and a benevolent feeling towards those
miserable beings who filled the laborious situations
of life, would have been considered the extremity
of weakness and folly. "They showed no mercy
to the widow, did no good to the fatherless, nor
helped any man in his distress."[5] To accomplish

[5] Baruch vi. 37, 38.

a favourite object, human life was sacrificed freely and without compunction or regret, as Pharaoh Necho sacrificed 120,000 men in a fruitless attempt to cut a channel from the Mediterranean to the Red Sea.

And if we refer to morality in a national point of view, the result will be exactly the same. Philosophers and hierophants gave public dissertations in praise of virtue, while they practised in private the most unbounded licentiousness. The morality of the Pagans in India may be estimated from the Bayaderes or dancing girls, who were the property of the priests; and the public worship of the Lingam;—that of Greece and Rome by the excesses of the Dionysiaca, and the prostitution of virgins in the temple of Mylitta;—while the nations of northern Europe and America were addicted to the sacrifice of human victims, and believed the practice to be a service well pleasing to God.

It is evident, therefore, that if we would apply the last definition to the ages which were past at the advent of Christ; we must reject the first member of the sentence, and leave out the allusion to morality. Its practice is indeed cosmopolite, and it was lauded amongst every description of people, but its object was mistaken, and consequently true morality—the love of God and of our neighbour, and the practice of every moral and social virtue—was unknown. But the remainder of the definition applies with great propriety to the

ancient mysteries of every country in the world,
which were truly veiled in allegory, and illustrated
by symbols. The former consisted in a description
of the reputed death of a celebrated individual who
was indifferently named Osiris, or Bacchus, or
Adonis, or its equivalent in every other nation;
with the ceremony of discovering the lost remains,
and raising them to a more decent interment.
The same legend with precisely the same reference,
formed the basis of the Spurious Freemasonry, in
every quarter of the globe.

10. The following, with which I conclude this
portion of the subject, can scarcely be termed a
definition of masonry. It is rather a general ad-
monition respecting the practice of religion, which
has been introduced into the ancient charges for
the express purpose of showing the cosmopolitical
nature of the institution. " In ancient times the
Christian masons were charged to comply with
the Christian usages of each country where they
travelled and worked; but masonry being found
in all nations, even of divers religions, they are
now only charged to adhere to that religion in
which all men agree (leaving each brother to his
own particular opinions) by whatever names, religions, or persuasions they may be distinguished;
for they all agree in the three great articles Noah,
enough to preserve the cement of the lodge. Thus
masonry is the centre of their union, and the
happy means of conciliating persons that otherwise must have remained at a perpetual distance."

This latitudinarian principle is well adapted to a society which is considered to be universal. It is expressed in such general terms as to be no burden upon any man's conscience, because it meddles with no system of religion, and leaves every member at full liberty to follow that way of faith in which he had been educated.

The modern lectures have rather encroached upon this universal principle by the introduction of subjects which bear a direct and exclusive reference to christianity. The historical Landmarks of masonry, as laid down in the lectures which are enjoined by authority in the 19th century, are, many of them, types of the christian religion; and they cannot be otherwise explained. And in a christian lodge, they either refer to christianity or nothing. In a Jewish lodge, our Hebrew brethren would interpret them differently, if they form a portion of their lectures, which is somewhat doubtful; and we are quite certain that in a Turkish lodge they would be carefully excluded. It is clear therefore that the lectures of masonry are arbitrary; and, with the exception of a few determinate Landmarks, vary essentially in different countries; being constituted in such a manner as to agree with the peculiar habits and belief of the fraternity who use them ; that the introduction of no startling facts or unacceptable doctrines, may cause disputes or divisions to arise amongst a brotherhood who profess to be cemented by the indissoluble chain of Brotherly Love.

The cosmopolitical construction of masonry may be also verified by the reputed extent of the lodge, which in length, and breadth, and depth, and height, is a representation of the universe as the temple of the living God. Thus the Lectures of masonry teach that "the universe is the temple of the deity whom we serve;—wisdom, strength, and beauty are about his throne as the pillars of his work; for his wisdom is infinite, his strength is omnipotent, and beauty shines forth throughout all creation in symmetry and order; he hath stretched forth the heavens as a canopy, and the earth he planted as his footstool; the canopy of his temple is crowned with stars as with a diadem; the sun and moon are messengers of his will, and all his law is concord."

In this quotation from the old lectures of masonry we find that a mason's lodge is a symbol of the universe, which is the magnificent temple of the deity, or the centre of the divine circle. But where is the circumference? This we are totally ignorant of. The centre however is sufficient for our present purpose, for it fills all known space, and extends throughout extent. The centre of the Almighty circle which the deity alone can fill, occupies millions upon millions of miles, farther than the human eye can reach, with all the assistance which the most improved instruments are able to afford. Sir John Herschel, in his "Essay on the power of the Telescope to penetrate into Space," a quality distinct from the magnifying power, in-

forms us that there are stars so infinitely remote
as to be situated at the distance of twelve millions
of millions of millons of miles from our earth; so
that light, which travels with a velocity of twelve
millions of miles in a minute, would require two
millions of years for its transit from those distant
orbs to our own, while the astronomer, who should
record the aspect or mutation of such a star, would
not be relating its history at the present day, but
that which took place two millions of years gone
by.

So universal is masonry. All mankind are
creatures of the same God, and equally the objects
of his care. He makes his Sun to shine upon the
evil and the good alike, and sendeth rain on the
just and unjust, for there is no respect of persons
with him. Thus also in Freemasonry " a king is
reminded that though a crown may adorn his head
and a sceptre his hand, the blood in his veins is
derived from the common parent of mankind, and
is no better than that of his meanest subject. The
statesman, the senator, and the artist, are there
taught that, equally with others, they are by nature
exposed to infirmity and disease; and that an
unforeseen misfortune or a disordered frame, may
impair their faculties, and level them with the
most ignorant of their species. Men of inferior
talents, who are not placed by fortune in such exalted stations, are instructed by masonry to regard
their superiors with respect, when they behold
them voluntarily divested of the trappings of ex-

ternal grandeur, and condescending, in a badge
of innocence and bond of friendship, to trace
wisdom and to follow virtue, assisted by those
who are of a rank beneath them. Virtue is true
nobility, and wisdom is the channel by which
virtue is directed and conveyed. Wisdom and Virtue alone, mark distinction amongst masons."

From all these arguments and demonstrations we
conclude that masonry is an institution which is
applicable to all mankind, in all ages and conditions of humanity; and its construction is so
perfect, that, although it has been strictly scruti-
nized, by enemies as well as friends, yet, notwithstanding the existence of a few anomalies, from
which no human establishment is free, no material
flaw has hitherto been found, of sufficient importance to endanger its existence. It has outlived
the envy of its opponents, and gathered strength
from every hostile attack. In some countries
Church and State have been arrayed against it
without effect;—demagogues and adventurers have
endeavoured to obscure its purity by heaping upon
it every kind of absurd innovation; but their respective systems, after an ephemeral existence have
sunk, one after another, into merited oblivion,
leaving Freemasonry to enjoy its triumph;—se-
ceders have threatened to betray its secrets, but all
their attempts have signally failed. The order
being based on Brotherly Love and Charity, is
imperishable. "Masonic secresy," says brother
Blanchard, a learned transatlantic mason, "is a

D

mysterious thing—it has never been divulged. The most tattling man, if he be a mason, keeps the secret. There is no risk of him. Enrage, discipline, expel—he never tells! Mad, drunk, or crazy—he never tells! Does he talk in his sleep? It is not about masonry. Bribe him in his wants—tempt him in his pleasures—threaten him, or torture him, he will endure being a martyr, but—he never tells!" All that have opposed its progress have shared the same fate, being met by the obloquy and derision of mankind."

CHAP. II.

THE LODGE.

The secunde artycul of good masonry,
As ye mowe hyt here hyr specyaly,
That every mayster, that ys a mason,
Most ben at the generale congregacyon,
Where that the semblé schal be holde ;
And to that semblé he most nede gon,
But he have a resenabul skwsacyon,
Or but he be unboxom to that craft,
Or with falssehed ys over raft,
Or ellus sekenes hath hym so stronge,
That he may not come hem amonge ;
That ys a skwsacyon, good and abulle,
To that semblé withoute fabulle.

ANCIENT MASONIC MANUSCRIPT.

I have often admired the observation of Plutarch, when treating on mental tranquillity. "That saying of Diogenes," he remarks, "extremely pleaseth me, who, seeing some person dressed very neatly to attend a public entertainment, asked him whether every day was not a festival of a good man? And certainly, that which makes it more splendid is— sobriety. For the world is a spacious and beautiful temple, which a man is brought into as soon as he is born, not to be a dull spectator of the works of art; but of things of a more sublime nature, which

D 3

have the principles of life and motion in themselves; such as the sun, moon, and stars; rivers, which are constantly supplied with fresh accessions of water; and the earth, which with the indulgence of a tender mother, suckles the plants, and nourishes her sensitive creatures. If life therefore is the most perfect institution to which we are introduced, it is but just that it should be passed in cheerfulness and tranquillity."

In like manner, when a candidate is first introduced into a lodge, which is a lively type of the world, he must not be an inattentive spectator, if he desires to reap any benefits from his initiation. He must, "read, mark, learn, and inwardly digest," all he sees, for everything which is visibly displayed before his eyes is invested with a moral signification, that may be beneficially applied to some useful purpose of civil, social, or religious life. The lessons of virtue which are drawn from these sensible objects are of the utmost value, because they are applicable to all views and circumstances; and they are extremely pleasing and attractive, because they are dictated in a spirit of kindness and cheerful benevolence.

The earliest description of a Lodge that I have met with explains it as being "just and perfect by the numbers 3, 5, and 7." This was subsequently exemplified in the following prescribed form. " A lodge of masons is an assemblage of brothers and fellows met together for the purpose of expatiating on the mysteries of the craft ; with the Bible,

Square, and Compasses, the Book of Constitutions, and the Warrant empowering them to act." In the formula used in the present day a further amplification has been adopted. It is here denominated "an assembly of masons, just, perfect, and regular, who are met together to expatiate on the mysteries of the order;—*just*, because it contains the volume of the Sacred Law unfolded ;—*perfect*, from its numbers, every order of masonry being virtually present by its representatives, to ratify and confirm its proceedings ;—and *regular*, from its warrant of constitution, which implies the sanction of the Grand Master for the country where the lodge is held." Some distinguish between the Charter, Warrant, and Constitutions, which indicate the regularity of a lodge; the first includes the sanction of the mysteries, forms, and ceremonies enjoined by the laws of the country where the lodge is assembled;—the second is the ancient and lawful authority of the Grand Master;—and the third is the sanction of the Grand Lodge. In the middle of the last century the Lodge was described as "a representation of the world, in which, from the wonders of nature, we are led to contemplate the Great Original, and worship him for his mighty works ; and for the same reason we are also moved to exercise those moral and social virtues which are incumbent on mankind as the servants of the Great Architect of the Universe, in whose form they were created."

The above definitions combined will show that a lodge of masons is a school for the practice of

science and good manners; and a microcosm, or
representation of the universe. From a principle
of piety to the Most High, its pursuits lead to a
knowledge of virtue both moral and social, and
the exercise of those courtesies which produce confidence and mutual esteem betwixt man and man.
In form and extent it is an oblong square ; its
length reaching from east to west, its breadth from
north to south, its height, according to the most
ancient definition, "inches, feet, and yards innumerable, extending to the heavens;" and its depth
"to the centre of the earth;" which, in a globe or
sphere, is the greatest extent that can be imagined.
This universality was symbolized by the Theo-
sophical masons of the last century, as the "Heart
of God in the centre of a cross, signifying the
trinity in a globular Rainbow, wherein the *red*, sig-
nifies the Father's property in the glance of fire ;
yellow the Son's lustre and majesty; *blue*, the sub-
stantiality; the dusky *brown*, the kingdom of darkness. On such a Rainbow will Christ sit to judge;
and thus is he undivided every where, and in that
man who is born of God, is the whole undivided
Heart of God, the Son of Man, sitting in the circle
of his life upon the Rainbow at the right hand of
God; for that man is Christ's member, his body,
his brother, his flesh, his spirit;—power, majesty,
heaven, paradise, elemental stars, earth and all, is
that man's who in Christ is above hell and devils,
though his earthy life be under heaven, stars,
elements, hell and devils."

The lodge stands " on holy ground ;" having been consecrated by three offerings on the spot where Solomon's temple was erected ; all of which were distinguished by the visible appearance of the Angel Lord of the Covenant—Jehovah—the Messiah, or Christ, as types of his presence on the same mountain to work out human salvation by his death upon the cross. It is placed, according to the testimony of the old York Lectures, " on the highest hill or in the lowest vale ; in the valley of Jehoshaphat or any other secret place ;" that if a cowan, or intrusive listener should appear, the Tyler might announce the fact by the usual report ; and the Master, being thus cautioned, the business of the lodge might be suspended till enquiry were made into the causes of the interruption ; and in case of actual danger, the Jewels might be put by, the Lodge closed, and the brethren dismissed to their respective homes. This exclusive principle was used by the Essenes and the early christians in times of hot persecution, when they were reduced to the alternative of either abandoning their religion, or celebrating its rites in secret crypts and caverns. The same custom was resorted to by the Freemasons in the middle ages, but with a different purpose. Their design was not to practice forbidden rites, but to guard the secrets of their art from the knowledge of the profane ; and it is well known that in the earliest era of the masonic establishment, a geometrical figure, or canon, was adopted in all sacred buildings, which had an import hidden from the vulgar. It was called the Vesica Piscis; and had a decided reference to the christian religion, and also an equal analogy with other mysteries professed by the first society of masons.[1] For the purposes of these meetings, crypts and secret conclaves were constructed, where the lodges were always held.

The pavement of a lodge is mosaic—the opus Grecanicum of the ancients—skirted with the "indented Tarsell," or tesselated border. These little lozenge-like tessaræ, being alternately white and black, refer to the quick recurrence of pleasure and pain, happiness and misery, by which this life is diversified; the white squares representing virtue and happiness, and the black ones vice and misery. Indeed the designs of Providence could scarcely be accomplished in the absence of such a wise dispensation. The nature of man is so very imperfect, that uninterrupted ease and enjoyment would introduce presumption and impiety, and terminate in destruction. It was from such considerations as these that our Royal Grand Master confessed, " It is good for me that I have been afflicted, that I might learn the statutes of the Lord." Affliction and pain are sent to us as friends and correctors; for " whom God loveth he chasteneth." In a word, without affliction we should never become master of that valuable masonic precept which teaches us to know ourselves, and to do to others as we would have them do to us.

1 Dallaway. Archit. p. 418.

The equal distribution of the tesseræ in our Mosaic pavement would seem to imply that virtue and vice are equally spread over the face of the earth. A moral writer of the last century however disputes the fact, and I am inclined to agree with him. He says, "whatever be the sum of misery in the world, there is a much larger sum of happiness. The weather is sometimes foul; but it is oftener fair. Storms and hurricanes are frequent; but calms are more common. There is some sickness; but there is more health. There is some pain; but there is more ease. There is some mourning; but there is more joy. There is complexional depression that asks—wherefore is light given to him that is in misery?—but it bears no proportion to the native cheerfulness which is open to the agreeable impressions of surrounding nature. Multitudes have been crushed under the foot of cruelty; but greater multitudes have remained unmolested by the oppressor. Many have perished with hunger and nakedness; but more have been supplied with food and raiment. If we thus survey the chequered face of human life at large, we shall find its bright spaces more numerous than its shadows."

This conclusion has been formed under the influence of christianity. Other religions entertain a more melancholy view of the state of human nature. "I have heard," says Lane,[2] "Arabs confess that their nation possesses nine-tenths of

[2] Arabian Nights, vol. i. p. 125.

the envy that exists among all mankind collectively. Ibn Abbas assigns nine-tenths of the intrigue or artifice that exists in the world to the Copts; nine-tenths of the perfidy to the Jews; nine-tenths of the stupidity to the Maghrabees; nine-tenths of the hardness to the Turks; and nine-tenths of the bravery to the Arabs. According to Kaab El-Ahbar, reason and sedition are most peculiar to Syria; plenty and degradation to Egypt; and misery and health to the Desert."

Freemasonry teaches her children, through the medium of the symbolical floor of the lodge, to observe the diversity of objects which beautify and adorn the creation, the animate as well as the inanimate parts thereof. The Blazing Star in the centre, refers us to that grand luminary the Sun, which enlightens the earth by its benign influence, and dispenses its blessings to mankind in general; giving light, life, and motion, to all things here below. The indented Tarsel, or tesselated border, refers to the planets in their several revolutions, which form a beautiful skirtwork round the Sun, as the other does to the pavement of a mason's Lodge.

The ornamental crown of the lodge is its cloudy canopy, which is accessible by a series of steps called the Ladder of Jacob, that reaches to the heavens, and rests on the volume of the sacred law; because, by the doctrines contained in that holy book, we are taught to believe in the wise dispensations of Providence; which belief strength-

ens our *faith* and enables us to ascend the first
step. This naturally creates in us a hope of becoming partakers of the promises therein recorded;
which *hope* enables us to ascend the second step.
But the third and last being *charity*, comprehends
the whole, and the mason who is possessed of that
virtue in the amplest sense, may justly be deemed to
have attained the summit of his profession; figuratively speaking to an ethereal mansion veiled from
mortal eye by the starry firmament, and emblematically depicted in a mason's lodge by seven
stars, which have an allusion to as many worthy
brethren, regularly initiated, passed, and raised,
without which number no lodge is esteemed perfect, nor can any gentleman be legally initiated
into masonry within its walls.

The altar of the lodge is a pedestal in the form of
a double cube, on which is displayed the holy
bible to confer upon it the attribute of justice.
And why is the open bible said to be the emblem
of justice? I answer in the expressive words of an
eloquent writer, because there is no other virtue of
such absolute importance and essential necessity
to the welfare of society. Let all the debts of
justice be universally discharged; let every man
be just to himself and to all others; let him endeavour, by the exercise of industry and economy,
to provide for his own wants, and prevent himself
from becoming a burden upon society, and abstain,
in the pursuit of his own subsistence, from every
thing injurious to the interests of others; let every

one render unto all their due—that property which he is obliged by the laws of the land or by those of honourable equity, to pay them; that candour and open dealing to which they have a right, in all his commercial intercourse with them; that portion of good report to which their merit entitles them; with that decent respect and quiet submission which their rightful civil authority demands. If justice were thus universally done, there would be little left for mercy to do. The universal discharge of this one duty would produce, in human life, a picture of happiness that would content the eye of charity. Generosity would have only to spread a heightening colour over, and breathe a richer spirit into the piece. The acts of Justice are the pillars of society; if they stand firm, undefaced, and fair, charity will have only to beautify the capitals of the eternal columns, and lend a little ornament to the well supported fabric. Let mankind be left to themselves without molestation; to the unimpeded operations of their own powers; to the goodness of nature and of God; and pity will have few tears to shed; friendship few words of comfort to utter; and beneficence but few offices of relief to perform.

The fixed lights of the lodge were formerly represented by "three windows supposed to be in every room where a lodge is held; referring to the cardinal points of the compass, according to the antique rules of masonry." There was one in the

East, another in the West, and another in the South, to light the men *to*, *at*, and *from* labour; but there was none in the north, because the sun darts no rays from thence. These constitute the symbolical situations of the three chief officers. Hence our transatlantic brethren affirm that " a lodge is, or ought to be a true representation of king Solomon's temple, which was situated north of the ecliptic; the sun and moon therefore, darting their rays from the south, no light was to be expected from the north; we therefore, masonically, term the north a place of darkness." The W. Master's place is in the East; to call the brethren *to* labour; the J. W. is placed in the South, to cheer and encourage them *at* their work; and the S. W. in the West, to dismiss them *from* their daily toil. And the lodge was so constructed that if a cowan was caught listening or prying into the business of masonry, he was punished by " being placed under the eaves in rainy weather, to remain exposed to the droppings till the water ran in at his shoulders, and out at his heels." [3]

The above description of a mason's lodge will be found to embrace a perfect picture of the universe, both in its attributes and its extent. The sun governs the day, the moon the night, and the stars illuminate the spangled canopy of heaven; while the earth is spread with a carpet of natural mosaic work, beautiful to the eye, and administering to the necessities of man. The hills are

[3] Old Lectures.

adorned with flocks and herds; the valleys stand
thick with golden grain; the parterres of nature
are covered with fragrant flowers and nutritive
herbage. " He watereth the hills from above;
the earth is filled with the fruit of his works. He
bringeth forth grass for the cattle; and green herb
for the service of men; that he may bring food
out of the earth, and wine that maketh glad the
heart of man, and oil to make him a cheerful countenance, and bread to strengthen man's heart." [4]
The ocean flows round it as a beautiful skirtwork
or tesselated border, not merely as an ornament,
but as a medium of communication between distant
countries, and a gigantic reservoir for the. production of food, " wherein are things creeping
innumerable, both small and great beasts." The
cloudy canopy is a symbol of heaven, and the steps
which lead to it are the innumerable emanations
from the three Theological virtues, Faith, Hope,
and Charity.

[4] Psalm civ. 13, 14, 15.

CHAP. III.

THE RITUAL OF BUILDING.

Every towere bretered was so clene
Of chose stone, that were far asundre ;
The workmen have with fell and sterne visages
Of riche entayle
Wrought out of stone, and never like to fail,
And on each turrett were raised up figures
Of savage beasts.

LIDGATE.

SUCH is the design and such the uses of a mason's Lodge. But before it arrives at this perfection, many preliminary ceremonies are necessary. If an oblong building be erected for the purposes of a barn or warehouse, it never changes its character, but remains a barn or warehouse to the end of its days. But if the same edifice be constructed for a mason's lodge, the rites of building, dedication, and consecration, convey to it a higher destiny. It then becomes a place where science is taught, and the precepts of morality and virtue are unfolded; and by the influence of its ornaments, furniture, and jewels, it acquires a solemnity of character, and a devotion of purpose, that excite veneration, and give it an aspect of

E 3

holiness even in the opinion of the most casual
visitor, who, though not a mason, may be incited
by curiosity to inspect its internal arrangements,
and speculate upon the uses of the various symbols and regalia which are disposed with such
order and regularity within its walls.

Freemasonry is an institution of ceremonies.
Every point, part, and secret which it contains, is
hedged about with forms that preserve it from the
prying eyes of the uninitiated on the one hand,
and from deterioration in its transmission from
age to age amongst ourselves, on the other. This
attachment to ceremonial observances is by no
means either singular or of modern invention.
Their use was dictated by the divine example at
the creation;[1] sanctioned on the same authority,
by the practice of the patriarchs, and the elaborate
ordinances of the Jewish church; and at length
introduced into christianity by the command of its
founder, and the precepts and admonitions of his
holy Apostles. Thus St. Paul, speaking to the
Corinthians on the ceremonies of the church, which
had been violated by the introduction of new and
unauthorized innovations, said, " Let all things be
done decently and in order."[2] His admonitions on
this head are extremely comprehensive, and embrace a series of observances which were dictated
by inspiration, and intended to be binding on
christians to the end of time. On this subject the

[1] See the Historical Landmarks of Masonry, vol. i. p. 494.
[2] 1 Cor. xiv. 40.

Church of England is eloquent. She says, "without some ceremonies it is not possible to keep any order or quiet discipline; and therefore we think it convenient that such ceremonies should be used as are best to the setting forth of God's honour and glory, and to the reducing of the people to a most perfect and godly living." [3]

As the use of ceremonies was considered necessary in a church divinely founded; how much more in an institution like that of Freemasonry, is it necessary and appropriate to confer beauty and solidity on the system. Ceremonies, however, considered abstractedly, are of little value, except they contribute their aid to impress upon the mind scientific beauties and moral truths. And I will undertake to affirm that our system, complicated as it is, does not contain a single rite that is barren of intellectual improvement; and they all bear a reference to corresponding usages contained in the book which is always spread open on the pedestal of a mason's lodge. Bishop Sanderson makes them the test of obedience. He says, " let Ceremonies be as very trifles as any man can imagine them to be ; yet obedience sure is no trifle. They mistake the question when they talk of pressing ceremonies. It is Obedience, formally, that is required ;—ceremonies not otherwise pressed than as the matter wherein that obedience is to be exercised. If a master appoint his servant to do

[3] Introduction to the Book of Common Prayer. Of Ceremonies.

E 5

some small matter that he thinketh fit to have done, though of itself of no great moment, yet he will expect to be obliged; and it is great reason he should. If in such case the servant should refuse to do the thing appointed, because he had no mind thereunto, and should receive a check or correction for such refusal; could he sufficiently excuse his own fault, or reasonably complain of his master for dealing hardly with him by saying —the thing was but a trifle. Is it not evident that the thing which made the master angry, and the servant an offender in that case, was not precisely and formally, the leaving of the thing undone, which, had it not been commanded, might have been left undone without any fault or blame at all, but the refusing to do it when he that had a right to his service commanded him?"[4]

Ceremonies are considered of such importance amongst masons, as sometimes to be exhibited to the dead; but these are not proper to be publicly expatiated on, because they apply to such brethren only as have acquired a competent knowlege of the art; and are never displayed but in the most secret recesses of a closely tiled lodge, and during the solemnization of a peculiar rite which none but Master Masons know. The ceremonies of masonry commence before the footstone of the lodge is deposited in the ground; and this is also accompanied by peculiar forms which consecrate

[4] Preface to Bishop Sanderson's Sermons.

the proceedings, and invest them with importance in the estimation of the public.

When the erection of a Masonic Hall, or Lodge Room has been determined on, the first thing to be considered is the Plan, which is a matter of the greatest importance; for the regularity of all the rites and ceremonies of the order depend, principally, upon the proper construction of the place of assembly. Our continental brethren are governed in this particular by a Ritual of Building, which it is venal to violate; and they feel a more than common interest in a punctual observance of the ordinances there prescribed, that their lodges may be erected, like horoscope of an expert astrologer, without the violation of any rule, even in the minutest particular; for as no correct decision respecting the native's destiny can be elicited from an informal figure of the heavens; so our continental brethren believe that the efficacy of Freemasonry will be considerably deteriorated, if there be any error or imperfection in the formation of the lodge where its benefits are imparted.

In this country, Masonic Halls are frequently erected at a great expence, and when finished, are deficient in many things which contribute to the effect of the ceremonies, and the comfort of the brethren. These evils will surely arise when an Architect is employed who is not a mason, and consequently ignorant of those especial accommodations which are indispensable to a good lodge; and which none but masons can appro-

priately introduce. Vitruvius tells us that the
Ephesians had a very wise law relative to the construction of public edificies. The architect whose
plan is chosen, enters into a bond by which he
engages to forfeit the whole of his property if the
building be not erected conformably thereto. If
he fulfils the condition of his agreement, honours
are decreed to him. If the expence exceeds the
estimate by only one quarter, the surplus was paid
by the party building ; but if it amounted to more
the architect was compelled to suffer the loss. It
requires not only a talented architect, but an experienced Freemason, to build a Lodge which shall
contain every requisite for the proper administration of all the ceremonies of the order. The
following directions may be useful, but they are
necessarily restricted in their application, because
it is a subject on which it is impossible to be fully
explicit on all points connected therewith.

First then, a Masonic Hall should be isolated,
and, if possible, surrounded with lofty walls, so as
to be included in a court, and apart from any
other buildings to preclude the possibility of being
overlooked by cowans or eavesdroppers; for Freemasonry being a secret society, the curiosity of
mankind is ever on the alert to pry into its mysteries, and to obtain by illicit means, that knowledge which is freely communicated to all worthy
applicants. As however such a situation in large
towns where masonry is usually practised, can
seldom be obtained, with convenience to the breth-

ren, the Lodge should be formed in an upper story; and if there be any contiguous buildings, the windows should be either in the roof, or very high from the floor. In the latter case, the altitude of the lower part of the window, as prescribed in the Helvetian Ceremonies, is five cubits, calculating by the masonic cubit of 18 inches, and measuring from the superficies of the floor within. The observance of this rule would effectually protect our mysteries from profanation, and assure the brethren of a perfect security in the performance of their secret ceremonies. These windows ought to be all on one side—the South, if practicable—and furnished with proper ventilators, that the brethren be not incommoded when pursuing their accustomed avocations, by the heat of the lodge. The utility of ventilation is known to all good masons; nor can a building be properly finished without these conveniences judiciously disposed.

The windows being placed at the above distance from the ground, will indicate, in some measure, the height of the room; which, to preserve a just proportion, must of course be lofty. The proper height, as prescribed by the ancient rituals, is 27 feet, corresponding with the dimensions of the Pillars in front of the Porch of Solomon's Temple, which had a mystical signification, and therefore, as we shall presently see, had an appropriate place assigned to them in the lodge. They were hollow, to contain the constitutional records, being of sufficient capacity for that purpose; the diameter

being 6 feet and the outer rim 4 inches thick.
Some think that the lodge room should be 32½
feet in height to accord with the entire altitude of
the Pillars including the plinths and capitals ; but
this would be out of all proportion ; and if the
principle be accounted orthodox, there is no reason
why the entire bases should be rejected, which
would make the room 54 feet in height, and constitute a monstrous absurdity.

The room should be furnished with a pitched
roof, open within, and relieved with an ornamental
framework of oak, or painted so as to resemble
that species of timber. It should be supported on
corbels running along the cornice, on which should
be engraven masonic ornaments, or the armorial
bearings of eminent masons in the Province where
the Hall is situated, as a memorial of their zeal
and activity for the general prosperity of the order.
In estimating the height, it is to be reckoned from
the surface of the floor to the extreme point of the
gable. The dimensions of the room in length and
breadth have not been authoritatively prescribed,
because they will depend in a great measure on
the situation of the lodge, or the space which is
assigned for its position ; and this will often be
extremely circumscribed in a large and populous
place, where building land is scarce and dear, or
the fund inadequate to any extensive operations.
But in all cases, a due proportion should be
observed in the several members of the fabric
wherever it is practicable, that no unsightly ap-

pearance may offend the eye, by disturbing that general harmony of parts which constitutes the beauty and excellence of every architectural production.

The principal entrance to the lodge room ought to face the East, because the East is a place of Light both physical and moral; and therefore the brethren have access to the lodge by that entrance, as a symbol of mental illumination; for as Polydore Virgil quaintly says, " the manner of turnyne our faces into the easte when wee praie, is taken of the old Ethnikes, whiche, as Apuleius remembereth used to loke eastwarde and salute the Sonne. We take it in a custom to put us in remembraunce that Christe is the sonne of righteousnes, *that discloseth secretes.*" The approaches to the lodge must be angular, for a straight entrance is unmasonic and cannot be tolerated. The advance from the external avenue to the East ought to consist of three lines and two angles. The first line passes through a small room or closet for the accommodation of visitors before they have proved their qualifications to be admitted into the Lodge, by signs, tokens, and perfect points of entrance; for strangers must be lodged somewhere, and it ought to be out of sight and hearing of the Lodge, because on examination it is possible they might prove impostors, and their claims be consequently rejected. At the extremity of this apartment there ought to be another angular passage leading to the tyler's room adjacent to the lodge ; and from thence, by another right angle, you are admitted

into the presence of the brethren with your face
to the Light, and stand prepared to salute the
W. M. So sacred are the proceedings of a lodge,
and such is their immeasurable distance from common observation and remark, that the door which
opens from the tyler's room into the Lodge should
be protected by a screen of thick moreen, or a
double entrance door, that nothing whatever which
passes in the lodge should be heard even in this
privileged apartment.

In every convenient place the architect should
contrive secret cryptæ or closets. They are of indispensable utility, but in practice are not sufficiently
attended to in this country. On the Continent
they are numerous, and are dignified with the
name of Chapels. Two of these apartments have
already been mentioned; (1) a room for visitors;
(2) the Tyler's room; added to which there ought
to be (3) a Vestry where the ornaments, furniture,
jewels, and other regalia are deposited. This is
called the Treasury or Tyler's conclave, because
these things are under his especial charge; and a
communication is usually made to this apartment
from the Tyler's room. There ought also to be
(4) a Chapel for preparations, hung with black,
and having only one small light placed high up,
near the ceiling; (5) a Chapel for the dead, furnished with a table, on which are a lamp, and
emblems of mortality; (6) the Master's conclave,
where the records, the warrant, the minutes, and
every written document are kept. To this room
the W. M. retires when the Lodge is called from

labour to refreshment, and at other times when his presence in the lodge is not essential; and here he examines the visitors, for which purpose a communication is formed between his conclave and the visitor's chapel. It is furnished with blue; and here he transacts the lodge business with his Secretary. The Ark of the Covenant is also deposited in this apartment. None of these closets should exceed 12 feet square; and may be of smaller dimensions according to circumstances. In the middle of the Hall there should be (7) a moveable trap door in the floor, 7 feet long and 3 or 4 broad, opening into a small crypt about 3 feet in depth; the use of which is known to none but perfect masons who have passed through all the symbolical degrees.

These conveniences having been arranged by the expert architect, and transferred to the Tracing Board for permanent reference; the next care of the Master is to make due preparation for the ceremony of commencing the building in peace and harmony, and consecrating the ground to the purposes of masonry by laying the foundation stone with all the usual formalities of the craft. In Germany this duty is discharged with the greatest care and circumspection; for it is considered inauspicious to omit any one ceremony, how trifling soever it may appear, which custom has rendered necessary on such an august occasion. A building committee is therefore appointed to make the preliminary arrangements, and nothing is done without its previous sanction.

F

CHAP. IV.

THE FOUNDATION STONE.

" Thus saith the Lord God, Behold, I lay in Zion for a
Foundation Stone, a tried stone, a precious corner stone, a
sure foundation ; he that believeth shall not make haste.
Judgement also will I lay to the line, and righteousness to
the plummet."—Isaiah.

The appointment of a favourable day for levelling the footstone, is a question which occupies
the serious attention of the building committee ;
for our ancient brethren, in the construction of
any magnificent edifice, whether civil or religious,
believed that the success of the undertaking de-
pended, in a great measure on the genial influence
of the time when the work was commenced. The
masonic days proper for this purpose, are from
the 15th of April, to the 15th of May ; and the
18th of April has been pronounced peculiarly
auspicious for laying the Foundation Stone of a
mason's lodge.

In this reference we find some remnant of the
superstitions of bygone ages, when a potentate
consulted his astrologers on the most fortunate
period for commencing any public enterprize.
According to Lane, who quotes from El-Is-hákee,

the Mahometans consider thursday and friday,
especially the latter to be fortunate; monday and
wednesday doubtful; sunday, tuesday, and satur-
day, especially the last, unfortunate. It is said
that there are seven evil days in every month;
viz., the third, on which Cain killed Abel; the
fifth, on which God cast out Adam from paradise,
and on which Joseph was cast into the well; the
thirteenth, on which God took away the wealth of
Job and the kingdom of Solomon, and on which
the Jews killed the prophets; the sixteenth, on
which God exterminated the people of Lot, trans-
formed the Jews into apes, and on which the Jews
sawed Zacharias asunder; the 21st, on which
Pharoah was born, and drowned; the 24th, on
which Nimrod killed 70 women, and cast Abraham
into the fire; and the 25th, on which a suffocating
wind was sent upon the people of Hood. On the
contrary, with us, friday is deemed an unlucky
period to undertake any important business. Thus
Fynes Moryson, in his Itinerary, speaking of the
king of Poland, in 1593, says, " the next day the
king had a good wind, but before this, because
they esteemed friday to be an unlucky day, had
lost many fair winds." And it still continues to be
a superstition amongst the working classes of this
country, that it is unlucky to be married on a
friday.

The above named time for laying the Foundation
Stone of a Masonic Hall however, appears to be
appropriate without any reference to a superstitious

custom; because nothing can be more consonant
with reason and propriety, than to commence a
building in the early spring, that the workmen
may have the whole summer before them to complete the undertaking advantageously, in order
that they may celebrate the cape stone with confidence and joy.

A Master and two Fellow Crafts, if there be a
dearth of workmen, or war, or famine, or distress,
may lawfully begin the work of building a Lodge;
but if none of these causes be in operation to im-
pede the undertaking, he ought not to proceed
with less than seven workmen, for reasons which
are evident to every brother, but cannot be re-
vealed. And seven days, at the least, before the
period which the building Committee have fixed
for the commencement of the work, the Master,
by the assistance of his Secretary, should communicate such intention to every Lodge in the
Province; having previously made his arrangements with the Provincial Grand Master. The
Masters of Lodges are expected, on such occasions,
to render their assistance, not only by being present
at the ceremony of laying the foundation stone,
but also "by furnishing a beam of cedar, syca-
more, or fir, to place in the roof, besides such other
voluntary offerings as may be most convenient to
themselves."

On the appointed day, the Lodges being all
assembled in some convenient place, the Provincial
Grand Lodge is opened in due form; and proof is

strictly required of every visitor that he is a mason,
and qualified to be present, and to assist at the
ceremonial. Visitors residing in the Province, not
being members of any Lodge, should have a well
known brother ready to testify that they have
been regularly initiated into the order. Masters of
Lodges ought solemnly to assure the Provincial
Grand Master, that the persons whom they present, really belong to their own company; because
at a great meeting, where many strangers are sure
to assemble together on such an important occasion,
unqualified persons might, if due caution were not
observed, succeed in imposing upon the lodge, and
the brethren be innocently led to forfeit their Obligation. Strangers, therefore, should not only be
strictly examined, but should also be required to
produce their Grand Lodge Certificate, so that no
doubts may remain on the mind of any of the
brethren respecting the regularity of their initiation,
and their indefeasible right to be present. They
will then take the stranger's place; which is at the
head of the procession; except they be Grand
Masters or Deputy Grand Masters of another
province, when the testimony of any brother that
they hold, or have held this high office, shall be
deemed a sufficient warrant for their admission;
and a high place in the procession is usually
assigned to them, at the pleasure of the Provincial
Grand Master.

Instructions respecting the ceremonial are delivered by the Provincial Grand Master, who then

F 5

demands to see the Warrant of the Building Lodge;
and being satisfied on this point and all others by
the usual enquiries, he proceeds to address the
brethren present to the following effect. " I
hereby, in the presence of all these Worshipful
Masters, Wardens, and Deacons, and of all these
Master Masons, worthy and diligent workmen of
our secret Craft, do ask of you, and of your company, if you know yourselves, at this time, to have
done anything contrary to the laws of masonry,
which has not been communicated to the provincial
authorities, and whereby you ought to be suspended from your work?

WORSHIPFUL MASTER.

We are all good masons at this very time.

PROVINCIAL GRAND MASTER.

Have you, amongst your company any brother
guilty of brawlings, strife, and disobedience, in
open lodge?

WORSHIPFUL MASTER.

We have none, Right Worshipful Sir.

PROVINCIAL GRAND MASTER.

Have you any brother, who, after open Lodge,
is guilty of drunkenness, common swearing, or
profane words?

WORSHIPFUL MASTER.

We have none, Right Worshipful Sir.

PROVINCIAL GRAND MASTER.

Have you permission to do this day's work?

WORSHIPFUL MASTER.

We have; and if it be your will and pleasure,
it shall be here communicated.

After this ceremony has been performed, the
Provincial Grand Master proceeds to say;

"Masters, Wardens, Deacons, and brethren;
all here is right and as it should be. I give you
joy of this day's work. It has begun in zeal—let
it end in charity and brotherly love. May all
masons help us in our present undertaking; and
let us give due honour to the Master and brethren
of the —— Lodge, No. — for wishing to raise a
Temple to Masonry. May the blessing of the
Most High rest upon it. May the new Lodge
increase in its prosperity; and may it be an asylum
to harbour the poor brethren, and console the
rich. Amen. So mote it be."

The Ark of the Covenant is now furnished by
the Stewards with the Volume of the Sacred Law;
and also with salt, clay, a pair of compasses, and
other masonic emblems; and they deliver the Veil
to the Provincial Grand Master, who sprinkles it
with essences. All the brethren present then
walk round the room in procession, preceded by
the purple, and from a basin of perfume, the Provincial Grand Master sprinkles them as they pass
by him, exclaiming

"May all our deeds be sweet and savoury!
May we be a refreshing odour to our poor and
worthy brethren; for Charity is as sweet as roses!"

The Lodge being now adjourned, the public
procession is formed; which will be found in a
subsequent page, arranged for a Province, in accordance with the form prescribed by the authority

of the Grand Lodge. The principles on which it is founded are precisely similar to the regulations of civil society; for although Freemasonry is undoubtedly a democratic institution, yet its degrees of rank are placed on the same scale of systematic gradation, as is used for the regulation of precedency in a state or kingdom.

It is an admitted principle in masonry that the post of honour is the last place in the procession; which is accordingly taken by the Grand, or Provincial Grand Master, if he be present; a Grand Tyler with a sword being placed on each side, and a Sword Bearer before him; the swords being drawn, and the scabbards left behind. The Sword Bearer is preceded by the Standard of the Grand Master or of the Province, as the case may be, flanked by the Stewards with wands. Next in precedence are his company of the Grand or Provincial Grand Lodge, according to their office, clothed in purple, with Jewels of gold, and preceded by a Tyler with his sword also drawn. Then follow the private lodges according to their numbers, each arranged in form; i. e. the brethren first; then the officers agreeably to their rank, the Master being the last person, who is attended by the banner of the lodge. Thus the W. M. of the oldest lodge will be placed immediately before the purple brethren; and if the Provincial Grand Master and his Staff be not present, he will then take precedence, or the last place in the procession.

On the Continent the Grand Master walks under a gorgeous canopy of blue, purple, and crimson silk, with gold fringes and tassels, borne upon staves painted purple and ornamented with gold, by eight of the oldest Master Masons present; and the Masters of private lodges walk under canopies of light blue silk with silver tassels and fringes, borne by four members of their own respective companies. The canopies are in the form of an oblong square, and are in length six feet, in breadth and height three feet, having a semicircular covering. The framework should be of cedar; and the silken covering ought to hang down two feet on each side. In the centre of the procession is carried the Ark of Alliance, covered with a veil of blue, purple, and crimson silk, in alternate stripes, by four of the most aged masons present, without regard to their rank in masonry.

When the procession moves onward to the place where the foundation stone is prepared to be levelled, the music should play some solemn air; for lively tunes are indecorous and unsuited to this stage of the proceedings. Pleyel's German Hymn, Haydn's National Anthem, Handel's Minuet in Samson, or a slow march would be considered appropriate.

Having arrived within a proper distance of the spot, the procession halts, the brethren open to the right and left, so as to leave room for the Grand Master to pass up the centre, he being preceded by his standard and sword Bearer, the

Grand Officers and brethren following in succession from the rear, so as to invert the order of procession. The Grand Master having arrived at his station on a platform, the brethren form themselves into a square round the stone, which is directed to be laid in the corner of the Amorites. An Ode is then sung; the Grand Chaplain repeats a prayer, and the Grand Treasurer having deposited the various coins of the realm, the cement is laid on the lower stone, and being spread with a silver trowel by the Grand Master, the upper one is let down slowly to solemn music. The Grand Master then descends to the stone, and proves that it is properly adjusted by the plumb, level, and square, which are delivered to him in succession by the three officers to whom they belong; after which the architect delivers to him the mallet, with which he gives three knocks upon the stone. When the operations are completed, the Grand Master makes an address to the assembly, in which he tells them, in such language as he may be pleased to use, that we are lawful masons, true and faithful to the laws of our country, and engaged by solemn obligations, to erect magnificent buildings, to be serviceable to the brethren, and to fear God, the Great Architect of the Universe ;—that we have amongst us, concealed from the eyes of all men, secrets which cannot be divulged, and which have never been found out ;—but that these secrets are lawful and honourable, and not repugnant to the laws of God or man. They were entrusted, in peace and hon-

our, to the masons of ancient times, and have been
faithfully transmitted to us ; and that it is our
duty to convey them unimpaired to the latest
posterity. Unless our craft were good, and our
calling honourable, we should not have lasted for
so many centuries, nor should we have been honoured with the patronage of so many illustrious
men in all ages, who have ever shown themselves
ready to promote our interests, and to defend us
against all adversaries. We are assembled here
to-day in the face of you all to build a house for
masonry, which we pray God may deserve to
prosper; by becoming a place of concourse for
good men, and promoting harmony and brotherly
love throughout the world till time shall be no
more.

The brethren all exclaim, " So mote it be."

The above detail has been adapted from the
rituals which are used in Germany, France, and
other continental nations ; but I have inserted
nothing which is inconsistent with our own practice ; or which might not be used in this country
without the slightest violation of the ordinance for
the above has been issued by our own Grand
Lodge ; and there are some points which I consider to be an improvement on our practice. I
subjoin the continental formula.

After the brethren have formed themselves into
a fellow crafts lodge round the foundation stone,
the architect is called for, who places himself in
front of the Grand Master, who whispers in his

ear something which all Master Masons know; on which the architect produces the plan of the building, which is inspected, and handed round amongst the brethren. An anthem is then sung; and the Grand Master calls for the working tools of a mason and anoints them with oil. He then delivers them to the W. M. of the building lodge, who hands them to the architect. The Grand Master then says; "W. M. of the —— Lodge, what will your lodge be like ?

The W. M. answers nothing, but lifting up his right hand points first the heavens, and then to the earth, and then extends his arms to their utmost limit.

GRAND MASTER.

That is a good plan, Worshipful Master; but have you nothing more to tell me ?

The W. M. makes no verbal reply to this question, but puts his right hand on his heart, and presses the fore fingers of his left hand on his lips.

GRAND MASTER.

The W. M. does well, brethren, let us copy his example.

Underneath the foundation stone the officiating Master places some grains of Wheat, with a few drops of Oil and Wine, along with the coins of the country. In addition to which the Grand Master throws in a spoonful of salt, which is his exclusive privilege. The mortar is then spread as already described, and the stone descends; which is adjusted, &c. as before, accompanied by the following dialogue.

GRAND MASTER.

W. M. of the —— Lodge, what is the proper Jewel of your office?

WORSHIPFUL MASTER.

The Square, Right Worshipful Sir.

GRAND MASTER.

Have you applied the Square to those parts of the stone that should be square?

WORSHIPFUL MASTER.

I have so applied it, and find it to be correct.

GRAND MASTER.

Brother Senior Warden what is the proper Jewel of your office?

SENIOR WARDEN.

The Level, Right Worshipful Sir.

GRAND MASTER.

Have you applied the Level to the stone?

SENIOR WARDEN.

I have done so, and find it to be correct.

GRAND MASTER.

Brother Junior Warden what is the proper Jewel of your office?

JUNIOR WARDEN.

The Plumb Rule, Right Worshipful Sir.

GRAND MASTER.

Have you applied that instrument to the several edges of the stone?

JUNIOR WARDEN.

I have taken the precaution to do so, and find the stone perfect? G

GRAND MASTER.

Having full confidence in your skill in the Royal art, it only remains that I finish the work. (Here he strikes three times with a mallet upon the stone.) May this undertaking be conducted and completed by the craftsman, according to the grand plan, in peace, harmony, and brotherly love.

The Grand Master, attended by the purple brethren then descends from the platform, and compasses the foundations of the building in solemn procession ; after which returning to his canopy, he anoints the foundation stone with fresh oil copiously, till it runs down on all sides, saying,

" As Jacob the son of Isaac, the son of Abraham, fled from the face of his brother Esau, going from Beersheba toward Haran, he tarried in a certain place all night where he slept on the cold ground, with a stone for his pillow in great discomfort. Here he had a vision of the gates of heaven, and when he awoke he anointed the stone on which he slept with oil, and named the place Beth El, or the House of God. In like manner I anoint this stone with pure oil, praying that in the building which may arise from it none but good men may enter, and men that fear God. Then may it truly be said, Behold how good and joyful a thing it is, brethren to dwell together in unity ! It is like the precious ointment upon the head, that ran down unto the beard, even unto Aaron's beard, and went down to the skirts of his clothing. Like as the dew of Hermon which fell on the hill

of Sion; for there the Lord promised his blessing
and life for evermore."

An Anthem is then sung, and the brethren return to the lodge from whence they set out.

It may be useful in this place to add a few words
on the custom of scattering corn, wine, and oil,
and salt, on the foundation, as the elements of
consecration; which appears to have been a custom
of great antiquity. Corn, wine, and oil, taken together, are a symbol of prosperity and abundance;
and refer in this case to the anticipated success of
the Lodge where they have been used, in promoting amongst its members the blessings of
morality and virtue, and by an increase of the
brethren, to disseminate amongst mankind, the
benefits resulting from Brotherly Love, Relief,
and Truth, that society in general may profit by
an infusion of the principles of masonry into every
class, and introducing a better feeling into the
whole mass. Thus, as a little leaven leaveneth the
whole lump, so all may become masons in practice,
although not masons by profession; and the general amelioration of society be produced by the
genial influence of masonic wisdom, goodness, and
truth.

Corn was a symbol of the resurrection, which
is significantly referred to in the third degree of
masonry. Jesus Christ compares himself to a corn
of wheat falling into the ground, as a symbol of
the resurrection. St. Paul says, the sower sows
a simple grain of corn, no matter of what kind,

which at its proper season rises to light, clothed in verdure. So also is the resurrection of the dead. The Apostle might, says Calmet, have instanced the power of God in the progress of vivification ; and might have inferred that the same power which could confer life originally, could certainly restore it to those particles which once had possessed it. It is possible he has done this covertly, having chosen to mention vegetable seed, that being most obvious to common notice ; yet not intending to terminate his reference in any quality of vegetation. We find the same manner of expression in Menu, who, discoursing of children says, " whatever be the quality of the seed scattered in a field prepared in due season, a plant of the same quality springs in that field with peculiar visible properties. That one plant should be sown and another produced, cannot happen ; whatever seed may be sown, even that produces its proper stem." All this reasoning serves to prove that corn is a correct symbol of the resurrection.

Wine is a symbol of cheerfulness and joy. Thus David, speaking of the divine beneficence, says, " He causeth the grass to grow for the cattle, and herb for the service of man, that he may bring forth the food out of the earth, and *wine that maketh glad the heart of man*, .and oil to make his face to shine, and bread which strengtheneth man's heart." Vineyards were plentiful in Palestine. It was indeed peculiarly a land of corn, and wine, and oil. Thus to show the abundance of vines which should fall to the lot of Judah in the partition of the promised land, Jacob, in his prophetic benediction, says of this tribe, he shall be found

> Binding his colt to the vine,
> And to the choice vine, the foal of his ass.
> Washing his garments in wine,
> His clothes in the blood of the grape.

The Jews planted their vineyards, says "the Investigator," most commonly on the south side of a hill or mountain, the stones being gathered out, and the space edged round with thorns, or walled in. The expression of "sitting every man under his own vine," which is used more than once in our scriptures, probably alludes to the delightful eastern arbours, which were partly composed of vines. Norden speaks of vine arbours as being common in the Egyptian gardens; and the Præenestine pavement in Shaw's Travels, gives us the figure of an ancient one. The expression is intended to refer to a time of public tranquillity and profound peace.

Oil was anciently considered the symbol of prosperity and happiness. The oil of gladness mentioned in the Jewish writings, was a perfumed oil with which the people anointed themselves on days of public rejoicing and festivity. Every thing that was appropriated to the purposes of religion in the tabernacle and temple, were all consecrated with oil. Kings and priests were anointed in the same manner. And our lodges, as temples consecrated to morality and virtue, are also hallowed by the application of corn, wine, and oil.

Our ancient brethren used salt as an emblem of consecration, because it was a symbol of Wisdom and Learning. Our Saviour says, " have salt in yourselves, and have peace one with another." And St Paul adds, " let your speech be always with grace, and seasoned with salt." Salt is also a symbol of perpetuity and incorruption. Thus the Jewish law is said to have been " a covenant of salt before the Lord." And again in another place, " the Lord gave the kingdom of Israel to David and to his sons, by a covenant of salt." A foreign writer, under the date of 1666, quoted by Brand, says, " the sentiments and opinions both of divines and philosophers, concur in making salt the emblem of wisdom and learning ; and that, not only on account of what it is composed of, but also with respect to the several uses to which it is applied. As to its component parts, as it consists of the purest matter, so ought Wisdom to be pure, sound, immaculate, and incorruptible ; and similar to the effects which salt produces upon bodies, ought to be those of wisdom and learning upon the mind. This rite of salt is a pledge or earnest of the study of good hearts, and of obedience and duty." The application of this meaning of the symbol to our society is not difficult, because our profession is to cultivate Wisdom, to maintain charity, and to live in harmony and brotherly love. And it is ordained that none can use salt in the consecration of a Lodge but the Grand Master, because he is, in a peculiar manner, the pillar of Wisdom. The following epigram was written when the tax was first laid upon salt about the middle of the last century.

> The emblem o'th' nation, so grave and precise,
> On the *emblem of wisdom* have laid an excise.
> Pray tell me, grave sparks, and your answer don't smother,
> Why one representative taxes another?
> The Commons on Salt a new impost have laid,
> To tax Wisdom too, they most humbly are pray'd;
> For tell me ye patrons of woollen and crape,
> Why the *type* should be fin'd, and the *substance* escape?

Salt has ever been distinguished as an emblem of hospitality. Thus the governors of the Provinces beyond the Euphrates, writing to king Artaxerxes, tell him that " they are salted with the salt of the palace ;" meaning that they have the right of maintenance there. Waldron in his description of the Isle of Man, says, " no person will go out on any material affair without taking some salt in their pockets; much less remove from one house, marry, put out a child, or take one to nurse, without salt being mutually interchanged; nay, though a poor creature be almost famished in the streets, he will not accept of any food, unless you join salt to the rest of your benevolence." We have a curious instance of the regard paid to salt as an emblem of hospitality and friendship in distant countries, related by Harmer from D' Her-

belot. " Jacoub ben Laith, who appears to have
been nothing more than a captain of banditti in
Persia, having broken into the palace of the prince,
and collected a very large booty; he was on the
point of departing, when his foot kicked against
something which made him stumble. Imagining
it might be something of value, he put it to his
mouth and found it to be a lump of salt. Upon
this, according to the superstition of the country,
where the people considered salt as a symbol and
pledge of hospitality, he was so touched that he
left all his booty, and retired without taking anything with him. The next morning, the risk they
had run in losing so many valuables caused a strict
enquiry to be made, and Jacoub being found to be
the person concerned, he frankly told the whole
story to the prince, by which he so effectually
gained his esteem that he took him into his service,
and he ultimately succeeded his master on the
Persian throne."

Salt was also a symbol of Fidelity. Whence
the propriety of its use amongst masons. It was
also an emblem of eternity and immortality; because it is not liable to putrefaction itself, and pre-
serves every thing that is seasoned with it from
decay. Reginald Scott, in his discourse concerning
Devils and Spirits, asserts that " the devil loveth
no salt to his meat, for that it is a sign of eternity,
and used by God's commandments in all sacrifices."
In like manner the science of Freemasonry may be
aptly symbolized by salt, because it is eternal and

will never decay. It has existed from the creation, and will remain a blessing to man till this earth is burnt up and the elements shall melt with fervent heat; and then Love universal shall exist for ever amongst the glorified fraternity of saints and angels.

CHAP. V.

THE DECORATIONS.

In which ther were mo ymages
Of gold standing in sondrie stages ;
In mo riche tabernacles ;
And with pierre moe pinnacles,
And moe curious pourtraytures
And quent mannere figures.
* * * * *
Of these yates flourishinges
Ne of compaces ne of kervings,
Ne how the hacking in masonries ;
As corbelles and imageries.

CHAUCER.

THE next ceremony by which the newly-built
hall is appropriated to masonic purposes is the disposal of its furniture and decorations preparatory
to the solemn rite of dedication and consecration.
Great discrimination is required to accomplish this
point correctly and with proper effect; and very
frequently the imposing appearance which a lodge
ought to present to the eye, is lost for want of due
attention to these preliminary arrangements. The
expert mason will be convinced that the walls of a
lodge room ought neither to be absolutely naked

nor too much decorated. A chaste disposal of
symbolical ornaments in the right places, and
according to propriety, relieves the dulness and
vacuity of a blank space; and though but sparingly
used, will produce a striking impression, and contribute to the general beauty and solemnity of the
scene.

The embellishment of the interior of a Lodge
room is indeed of vast importance; although I am
afraid, very little attention is usually paid to it;
and nothing but a fine and discriminating taste
can do it ample justice. Nor is it necessary to
incur heavy expences in the details, for it is the
design, and not the value of the materials, that
produces the effect. A few brief hints for this
purpose may be acceptable; although after all,
much will depend on the judgment of the architect, who ought, in all cases, to be a brother.

Over the row of windows, which, as I have
already observed, are disposed on one side of the
room, should be placed, running from east to west,
a thick brass rod, on which is suspended, from a
series of rings of the same metal, a great curtain
extending the whole length of the room, and
when drawn, covering all the windows at once,
for separate window curtains are unmasonic, and
not to be tolerated in a good lodge. This great
curtain must be composed of blue, purple and
crimson moreen, disposed in alternate stripes, the
breadth of the stuff, and lined with black cloth.
Silk may be used if the lodge be prosperous enough

to incur the expence, but neither cotton or linen
are allowed. It must, however, be quite plain and
devoid of ornament; for the intended effect would
be entirely destroyed by the introduction of tassels,
fringes, or binding of any other colour.

In the east should be a raised platform or dais
for the Master and his attendant officers. Here
are the two pillars already mentioned flanking the
Chair or Throne, which is elevated on three steps
at some distance from the wall; for sufficient
space ought to be left for two persons to pass conveniently, which is concealed from the observation
of the brethren by a screen placed behind the
chair, higher than the Master's head when seated.
The two extremities of the screen are made to fold
inwards at right angles, thus enclosing the officers
on the dais by three sides of a parallellogram. On
the back of the screen a design should be painted
on a ground of black or dark purple, emblematical
of the name of the lodge; and the flaps should be
decorated with intersecting triangles, emblems of
mortality, or other masonic designs according to
the taste of the architect. The effect will be
augmented by painting it as a transparency. In
foreign Lodges there is placed behind the throne,
and high up in the gable of the roof, a well toned
bell or Indian gong; and I have known it used
with good effect in our own country.

The pedestal is placed in front of the throne.
In form it is a double cube; and should be made
of shittim wood or acacia, in imitation of the Altar

of incense and other appendages to the tabernacle of Moses. This masonic altar is consecrated by the Book of the Law, which is always spread open upon it, at some important passage of scripture, during the continuance of the solemn ministrations of the lodge. In the first degree it is usually unfolded at Ruth iv. 7; in the second degree at Judges xxii. 6; and in the third at 1 Kings vii. 13, 14. These usages however, it may be necessary to add, are arbitrary; for we find, at different periods during the last century that Genesis xxii. and xxviii, were indifferently used for the first degree; 1 Kings vi. 7, and 2 Chronicles iii. 17, for the second; and Amos x. 25, 26, and 2 Chronicles vi. for the third. In the United States, according to the instructions contained in Cross's Chart, the Bible is opened in the first degree at Psalm cxxxiii; in the second at Amos vii; and in the third at Ecclesiastes xii.

Again, during the ceremony of consecrating a Lodge the Volume should be displayed at 1 Kings viii; in processions at Numbers x; and at funerals at Gen. i., or 1 Cor. xv. It is however, a matter of little importance, provided the passage correspond with the structure of any part of the degree. A section of our brethren have always evinced the greatest anxiety that this arrangement should be punctually observed; and are even so particular as to have the obligation sealed on the appropriate verse; while others treat it with indifference; and some care very little whether it be

wholly omitted. In fact I knew a lodge where the
Master always opened his Bible at Eccles. x,
which has no masonic reference whatever.

In the West, and facing the Master's Throne,
there ought to be a gallery furnished with an
organ; which is also useful for a musical band,
or for the accommodation of ladies on festive
occasions.

The technical ornaments of a lodge are, as is
well known, the mosaic pavement, the blazing
star, and the tesselated border; but a well disposed
lodge room admits of other ornaments which add
considerably to the brilliancy of its appearance.
These decorations, however, ought to be in the
strictest conformity with the genius of the order.
Their introduction is frequently the effect of accident. A cheap purchase at a sale, or the indiscriminate liberality of an individual brother, will
frequently place amongst the ornaments, a picture
or bust, which is not in keeping with the general
contour of the lodge furniture. Such anomalies
ought to be avoided.

The Freemason's Hall, Great Queen Street, is
a beautiful specimen of this kind of ornament, as
it was designed by the architect at the period of
its erection. It is purely masonic; and hence it.
is to be presumed that statues or paintings of the
Virtues are in good taste ; as also of the worthies
named in the Bible, who are celebrated in the
system of masonry; such as Abraham or Moses,
Solomon or H A B, or the two St. Johns; any or

all of these would be appropriate. Nor should pictures of the great benefactors of masonry be omitted, as a memento of departed worth which the craft delights to honour. These decorations, judiciously interspersed with masonic emblems, if properly managed, may contribute to produce a very imposing appearance. A marble slab, containing the name of the lodge, with its founder, and the contributors to the building fund, ought to be let into the north wall. The candlesticks should be made of brass, and very lofty. These add a grace to the appearance of a lodge which can only be estimated by those who have witnessed the effect. Some of the most gorgeous foreign lodges use a seven branched candelabrum, in imitation of the golden candlestick of the tabernacle and temple; and this appears to be a most appropriate article of furniture to occupy a conspicuous place in the lodge. It was a truly magnificent utensil, weighing 125 pounds, and therefore would be worth about £6000 of our money. It stood upon a base with a perpendicular stem, at the top of which was the centre light. Three branches projected from the stem on each side, forming the segment of a circle, and rising as high as the centre light. The whole of the candlestick was adorned with a variety of carved ornaments, all in chased gold. In a lodge the candlesticks should always be composed of bright brass; wood of all kinds being extremely improper.

H 3

In a good lodge silence and gravity are great recommendations during the hours appropriated to labour. The ordinary business is of too serious a nature to admit of any disturbances; and hence the ancient charges direct that no brother shall behave himself ludicrously or jestingly while the lodge is engaged in what is serious and solemn; nor use any unbecoming language upon any pretence whatever; but to pay due reverence to the Master, Wardens, and fellows, and put them to worship. Even the noise of moving the seats or the feet, is to be avoided as much as possible; and for this purpose sand is not allowed to be strewed on the floor; nor are the brethren permitted to leave the Lodge during the solemn ceremonies, lest the noise thus made should disturb the proceedings. The effect of an initiation would be entirely destroyed by any interruption of this kind; and it is easy to understand that the same kind of disturbance would be calculated to distract the attention of the brethren during the delivery of the lectures. It would also create a degree of embarrassment to the Master, and tend to disarrange his ideas, and consequently, to some extent, nullify his instructions. It is to prevent the occurrence of all such irregularities that the Grand Lodge have provided that " if any brother behave in such away as to disturb the harmony of the lodge, he shall be thrice admonished by the Master; and if he persist in his irregular conduct he shall

be punished according to the By-Laws of the
lodge ; or the case may be reported to higher
masonic authority." The best method of prevent-
ing any casual disturbance on the floor of the
lodge, is to have it covered with drugget or carpet-
ing ; and this is generally used in foreign lodges.

CHAP. VI.

THE NAME.

What's in a name? that which we call a rose
By any other name would smell as sweet.

SHAKESPEARE.

"The Phœnicians gave appellations to places according to
their respective commodities and manufactures, wherein, if we
do but seriously consider for what particular thing each country,
in former time, was most especially taken notice of, and then
apply the Phœnician name of that thing, let it be custom, situation, trade, or anything else, and we shall find the Phœnician
word so exactly agreeing with the nature of the country so expressed, that we must conclude it impossible so constant and
general an harmony between them should happen by chance;
but rather, that the names were imposed for some particular
reason or design."

SAMMES.

A word on the Names of lodges may not be
unacceptable. The brethren who drew up the
code of "the Helvetian Ceremonies of Masons,
said to come from Egypt, translated from the
French and German of L. S. U. and 2 B 7 C," condemn the use of such names as the Apollo, the
Minerva, the Vesta, &c., as being heathen, and
furnishing ideas of idolatry and superstition. They
also disapprove of the names which savour of any
sect or party, either religious or political. "These,"

they say, " can have nothing to do with masonry."
Des Etangs, however, contends that it is lawful
to use as the names of lodges, any of the great
heathen philosophers, such as Zoroaster, Confucius,
Pythagoras, Socrates, Plato, &c.; and also Wisdom, Good Faith, Friendship, Constancy, or any
other of the moral virtues.

In this country the titles of lodges are frequently
determined by chance; but the most appropriate
are those which are assumed from the names of
some ancient benefactor, or meritorious individual
who was a native of the place where the lodge is
held; as in a city, the builder of the Cathedral
Church; because it is quite certain that he was a
mason; for none but those who are impregnated
with the true scientific principles of the order,
could possibly have produced the mysterious and
complicated effect which those gorgeous edifices
uniformly display. The name of a Hundred or
Wapentake in which the lodge is situated, or of a
navigable river which confers wealth and dignity
on the town, are proper titles for a lodge; as are
also the orders of architecture, the theological or
cardinal virtues; and Harmony, Brotherly Love,
Friendship, Unity, or other social qualities of the
mind. In all cases the temper of the brethren
should correspond with the name of the lodge;
otherwise they will expose themselves to be ranked
as hypocrites, and instead of masonry constituting
their pride, it will subject them to obloquy and
shame. If the members of a lodge dedicated to

Friendship or Harmony be notoriously at variance with each other;—if the brethren of a lodge of Fidelity be, in practice, unfaithful to every trust; —if a lodge called Social Union be distinguished by bickerings and disputes; or of Good Faith, by defrauding or swindling their neighbours; what can be expected to result from such anomalies, but disorder amongst themselves and unpopularity in the world; their own character will be compromised, the lodge disgraced, and Freemasonry, which ought to be the vehicle of perfect friendship, will become a by-word and a reproach, in the estimation of all good and worthy men.

The precedency of lodges, however, depends on the Number and not on the Name; although by custom every lodge has its proper name; and this is considered of such importance by the masonic authorities, that the approbation of the Grand Master, or at least of the Provincial Grand Master must be obtained before any name can be legitimately used; and even then it must be registered with the Grand Secretary. Nor can any lodge alter its name without the same authority. The privilege of giving a name has always been considered as a token of authority. Thus a father is empowered to determine the names of his children, and a master those of his servants. For the same reason the Master determines the name of his lodge. It is said in Scripture that Adam gave a name to his wife and to all the animals, which they ever after retained. God himself condescended to

change the names of Abram, Jacob, and Sarai, as
a token of honor, and an addition expressing his
particular regard for them. Hence he gave a
name, even before their birth, to some persons to
whom he purposed to extend his favours in an
especial manner; as to Solomon whom he called
Jedidiah; to the Messiah whom he called Emanuel
and Jesus, to John the Baptist, &c.

Assigning a name to a lodge, like the deter-
mination of the name of a son or daughter, is
frequently a matter of much serious deliberation;
and is sometimes attended with powerful religious
feelings. "The strange prejudice of lucky and
unlucky names," says D'Israeli, " prevailed all
over modern Europe. The successor of Adrian
VI., wished to preserve his own name on the
papal throne; but he gave up the wish when the
conclave of Cardinals used the powerful argument
that all the Popes who had preserved their own
names, had died in the first year of their pontificate.
Cardinal Marcel Cervin, who preserved his name
when elected Pope, died on the twentieth day of
his pontificate, which confirmed this superstitious
opinion. La Moth le Vays gravely asserts that all
the queens of Naples of the name of Joan, and
the kings of Scotland of the name of James, have
been unfortunate; and we have formal treatises on
the fatality of particular names."

The same credulity still operates, to a certain
extent, amongst ourselves; and not only the
ignorant, but also men of learning and talent are

scarcely able to divest themselves of certain fancies
about the names of their children ; as if their
success in life were to be dependant on a casual
appellation imposed at the font. Nor is the superstition confined to any nation or people ; but
appears indigenous to the human mind. Amongst
the Romans there were certain mysterious notions
connected with the names of individuals. In
calling over a muster roll of soldiers, the serjeants
always began with names of good omen, as Felix,
Faustus, &c., analagous to our Good luck, Happy,
&c. Livy, speaking of a person named Atrius
Umber, calls it *abominandi ominis nomen ;* and in
like manner Plautus says of one whose name was
Lyco,

Vosmet nunc facite conjecturam cæterum,
Quid id sit hominis, cui Lyco nomen siet.

Plato recommended to parents to select lucky
names (fausta nomina) for their children ; and
Pythagoras thought a man's success in life was
dependant on his name. Camden has a story
illustrative of his feeling. " We reade that two
Ambassadours were sent out of France into Spaine
to king Alphonse the ninth to demand of the
daughters which he had by the daughter of king
Henrie the second of England, to bee married to
their soveraigne king Lewes the eighth. One of
these ladies was very beautifull, called Vrraca, the
other not so beautifull, but named Blanche. When
they were presented to the Ambassadours, all men
held it as a matter resolved that the choyce would

light upon Vrraca, as the elder and fairer. But
the Ambassadours enquiring each of their names,
tooke offence at Vrraca, and made choyce of the
lady Blanche, saying that her name would bee
better received in France then the other, as signifying faire and beautifull, according to the verse
made to her honour."

Candida, candescens candore, et cordis et oris.
And a modern French writer has the following
passage, which shows that the same feeling still
prevails amongst that people. " What is your
name, Mademoiselle ? Felise, replied the child.
It is a pretty name, said the kind hearted woman.
Felise—that means happy ; one that is born under
a fortunate star ! Hearing these words, the traveller and her attendant involuntarily turned, and,
doubtless struck by the same thought, cast a
singular look upon the child."

Pegge has quoted from Fuller an amusing instance of the same superstition in a Spaniard.
Such was the ridiculous attachment to long and
high sounding names and titles in Spain, that
when an epidemical sickness raged in London in
the reign of Queen Elizabeth, the Spanish Am-
bassador, who, I suppose, enjoyed a sesquipedal
name, was consigned for safety to the charge of
Sir John Cutts, at his seat in Cambridgeshire.
The don, upon the occasion expressed some dissatisfaction ; feeling himself disparaged at being
placed with a person whose name was so short.
An amnesty, however, was soon granted by the

Spaniard; for my author says, that what the knight lacked in length of name, he made up in the largeness of his entertainment."

When dramatic representations were first introduced into this country, the subjects were extracted from the Bible history; and the names of the patriarchs and saints were principally used, the devil being the chief comic performer. They were managed by the clergy, and enacted in churches and monasteries; or under their direction, in the public streets on Corpus Christi day. About the time of the Reformation, these Mysteries and Miracle Plays were rivalled and ultimately superseded by historical dramas called Moralities; and the names of the Virtues and Vices were substituted for scripture characters; the devil's place in Comedy being supplied by a personage named Ygnorance; whence was derived the Clown or Fool of Shakespeare and his contemporaries. These were secular Interludes, and the origin of the regular drama. Thus, in 1520, we find "A new Interlude and a Mery, of the nature of the IV. elements;" which contained the following characters—the Messengere, Nature, Naturale, Humanytie, Taverner, Experyence, Studious, Desire, Sensuall Appetyte, and Ygnorance. In 1567, was printed by Thomas Purfoote, a new and Mery Enterlude called the Trial of Treasure;" with these names :—Sturdines, Contentation, Visitation, Time, Lust, Sapience, Consolation, the Preface, Just, Pleasure, Greedy Gutts, Elation, Trust,

Treasure, and the Vice, who is here called Inclination. And to close these extracts, we find a multitude of curious names in a drama called Cambises, written by Thomas Preston about the same period; viz. Councell, Huf, Lob, Ruf, Commons Cry, Commons Complaint, Venus, Snuf, Small Hability, Proof, Execution, Diligence, Crueltie, Hob, Preparation, Ambidexter, Triall, Meretrix, Shame, Otian, and many others.

From this personification of the Virtues, the custom of giving similar names to children was greatly fostered and increased, in the hope that a propitious name might be the harbinger of virtue, prosperity, and happiness; whence the female names of Faith, Grace, Hope, Temperance, Charity, &c., abounded throughout England; and have become standard names, with which the poor as well as the rich daily flatter their own feelings by conferring them on their beloved offspring; and Freemasons usually follow the example in giving propitious names to their lodges.

I do not find, however, that our lodges had any distinctive names before the latter end of the last century. The four regular lodges which were found in practice in the south of England at the revival of masonry were designated by the sign of the taverns where they were respectively held. The same practice continued for many years. Before 1738, by an order of the Grand Lodge, an engraved list was published, which was received as occasion required. The two copies of this list

I

in my possession were respectively printed in 1764 and 1767; the former dedicated to Lord Blaney, G. M., and the latter to the Duke of Beaufort, G. M. In both cases the lodges are usually designated by a pictorial representation of the sign of the tavern where the brethren met. A printed list, dated 1774, appears to be in uniformity with those which were engraven. In 1784, Noorthouck published his edition of Anderson's Constitutions; and the laws of the Grand Lodge therein recorded, make no mention of the name of a lodge, but recognise the engraved list. In a catalogue dated 1790, the lodges have names as well as numbers; and two years later a list was published with names and numbers, as altered by the Grand Lodge. In the present Book of Constitutions the names of lodges are formally recognised, and directed to be enrolled in the Grand Lodge Books.

CHAP. VII.

THE CONSECRATION.

"And now the king's command went forth
Among the people, bidding old and young,
Husband and wife, the master and the slave,
All the collected multitudes of Ad,
Here to repair, and hold high festival."

SOUTHEY.

"All hail to the morning that bids us rejoice;
The temple's completed, exalt high each voice;
The Capestone is finished, our labour is o'er,
The sound of the gavel shall hail us no more.
Almighty Jehovah descend now and fill
This lodge with thy glory, our hearts with good will;
Preside at our meeting, assist us to find
True pleasures in teaching good will to mankind.
Companions assemble on this joyful day,
The occasion is glorious, the Keystone to lay;
Fulfil'd is the promise by the Ancient of Days,
To bring forth the Capestone with shouting and praise."

MASONIC CONSECRATION HYMN.

WE will now suppose the Lodge to be built, furnished, decorated, and named; it remains that the ceremony of Dedication and Consecration be performed before it can be legally used for masonic purposes; and that every thing may done decently and in order, these rites should be performed with

I 3

every fitting solemnity, and in due and ample form. The Worshipful Master having first made the necessary arrangements with the Provincial Grand Master, should instruct the Provincial Grand Secretary to make his preparations with the minutest accuracy, because the smallest omission may produce a very serious impediment in the ceremonial, and utterly destroy its effect. Much also will depend on the tact and activity of the Director of Ceremonies, whose duty it is to superintend the processions, and to see that every brother has his proper rank, according to the code of precedency which distinguishes the order.

It is usual on these occasions for the Provincial Grand Chaplain to preach a sermon at the church, to which the brethren move in formal procession. How trifling soever this may be considered by some inconsiderate persons, its regulation is the result of no ordinary management. To give it the proper effect requires the utmost nicety of arrangement. Every brother's place should be marked down on paper by the Director of Ceremonies, and openly proclaimed before he leaves the lodge to join his brethren in public. In the church, certain pews should be marked out as appropriated to the brethren according to their rank; others for ladies; and the rest for the miscellaneous congregation. Care should also be taken to prevent all ingress and egress during the celebration of divine service, by children or loose persons, who are attracted by curiosity, and feel no interest in the proceedings. In the course of my experience I have witnessed great disorders for want of a little preliminary caution in this respect. It should also be seriously impressed upon the Worshipful Master of every lodge, that he is responsible for the regularity and decorum of his Company; and that it is his duty to instruct and admonish them at some lodge of emergency to be convened at home for that especial purpose, on the necessity of appearing in the proper clothing of masonry; and on the conduct which it becomes them to observe at the approaching commemoration, that masonry in general, and their own lodge in particular may not suffer in the estimation of the public.

On the appointed day, the lodge having been opened in due form by the Provincial Grand Master, and the Minutes read and confirmed; the Provincial Grand Secretary is directed to read the order of procession; after which a charge is delivered from the throne on propriety of conduct, and the necessity of adhering strictly to all the forms, as they have been regulated by the masonic authorities. After which the lodge is adjourned, and the ladies are admitted into the gallery. The procession now moves round the lodge thrice, and afterwards the brethren remain stationary; the elements of consecration arranged, and the following passage from scripture is read by the Provincial Grand Chaplain.

" Then Solomon assembled the elders of Israel, and all the heads of the tribes, the chief of the fathers

I 5

of the children of Israel, unto king Solomon in Jerusalem, that they might bring up the Ark of the Covenant of the Lord out of the city of David, which is Zion. And all the men of Israel assembled themselves unto king Solomon at the feast, in the month Ethanim, which is the seventh month. And all the elders of Israel came, and the priests took up the Ark; and they brought up the Ark of the Lord, and the tabernacle of the congregation, and all the holy vessels that were in the tabernacle; even those did the priests and the Levites bring up. And king Solomon, and all the congregation of Israel that were assembled unto him were with him before the Ark, sacrificing sheep and oxen, that could not be told nor numbered for multitude. And the priests brought in the Ark of the Covenant of the Lord unto his place, into the oracle of the house, to the Most Holy Place." (1 Kings, viii. 1—6.)

An Anthem proper for the occasion is then sung, which is usually written for the purpose by some member of the lodge. The Architect then makes his report; and the Provincial Grand Master delivers a suitable Oration; and concludes by directing the brethren to move forward in procession to church.

This is the point when the talent of the Director of Ceremonies displays itself. Without the most judicious maragement on his part, a scene of great confusion would ensue. His duty is to place himself within the entrance of the lodge and proclaim

every brother by his office or rank as he is to take
his situation in the procession, beginning at the top
of his Roll, and suffer no person to pass, under
any pretence whatever, until his name be called.
This process, with an assistant below to arrange
the brethren as they arrive in the street, or in the
court of the lodge, as the case may be, will preserve due order, and complete the regularity of
the proceedings. To give facility to this move-
ment, the Masters of the several lodges should
act the part of captains of companies in a regiment
of soldiers on parade, and keep the brethren of
their respective lodges strictly together, not allow-
ing them to mix with other lodges ; because it
would occasion considerable embarrassment when
the names were called; and at this point of the
ceremonial no time ought to be wasted in re-
arrangement. Every lodge should be ready to
obey the summons of the Director of Ceremonies.

The following form of procession I should
recommend as being most appropriate for the use
of the Provinces ; every brother or file of brethren,
observing a distance of six feet in the rear of his
predecessor ; so that a procession of fifty brethren
walking by pairs may occupy a space of about
one hundred yards.

A Tyler with a sword.

Union Flag.

Band of Music.

Union Flag.

Visiting Brethren two and two.

Rough Ashlar borne on a pedestal.

Lodges out of the Province.

The private lodges of the County in the following order ; the highest numbers walking first.

Tyler with a sword.

Brethren two and two.

Inner Guard with a sword.

Two Deacons.

Stewards.

Secretary.

Treasurer.

Chaplain.

Past Master.

Two Wardens.

The Lodge Banner.

Master.

The Perfect Ashlar borne on a Pedestal before
the W. Master of the senior lodge by a brother of
his own Company.

P. G. Tyler with a sword.

Union Flag.

Tracing Board of the First Degree.

Inner Guard with a sword.

Past P. G. Deacons two and two.

Tracing Board of the Second Degree.

Past P. G. Organist.

Past P. G. Architect.

The two P. G. Deacons bearing the Warden's
Pillars on Pedestals.

A Cornucopia borne by a Brother.

P. G. Organist.

P. G. Architect.

P. G. Director of Ceremonies.

Tracing Board of the Third Degree.

Past P. G. Treasurer and Secretary.

The Book of Constitutions on a Pedestal.

P. G. Secretary.

P. G. Registrar.

P. G. Treasurer.

P. G. Steward with a wand. { The Holy Bible, Square and Compasses, carried by four Master Mason's Sons; open at Numbers x. } P. G. Steward with a wand.

P. G. Chaplain.

Past P. G. Wardens two and two.

The Three Lights placed triangularly on a Pedestal.

P. G. Junior Warden with a gavel.

P. G. Senior Warden with a gavel.

P. G. Steward with a wand. } P. G. Standard. { P. G. Steward with a wand.

The Globes on a Pedestal.

Banner of the D. P. G. M.

Deputy Provincial Grand Master.

P. G. Steward with a wand. } Banner of the P. G. M. { P. G. Steward with a wand.

P. G. Sword Bearer.

Tyler with a sword. } Provincial Grand Master. { Tyler with a sword.

Union Flag.

Two Stewards with wands.

P. G. Tyler with a sword.

When the procession arrives at the church door, the leading files halt, and the brethren fall back to the right and left as before mentioned, and make an opening for the Provincial Grand Master and his Staff to pass up the centre. Thus the procession will enter the church in a reversed order, and the Covenant is placed on a pedestal in front of the Reading Desk where it remains during the whole service.

On returning from church, the Lodge is resumed, and the dedication and consecration solemnized by an adherence to those ancient and secret forms which it would be improper as well as needless to describe here, as the outline, so far as can be legally communicated, may be found in Preston's Illustrations, and many other masonic works.

CHAP. VIII.

THE PILLAR OF WISDOM.

" The eleventhe poynt ys of good dyscrecyoun,
As ye mowe knowe by good resoun ;
A mason, and he thys craft wel con,
That sygth hys felow hewen on a ston,
And ys yn poynt to spylle that ston,
Amende hyt sone, yef that thou con,
And teche hym thenne hyt to amende,
That the werke be not y-schende.
And teche hym esely hyt to amende,
Wyth fayre wordes, that God the hath lende,
For hys sake that sytte above,
With swete wordes noresche hym love."

ANCIENT MASONIC MANUSCRIPT.

FREEMASONRY may be justly considered as a regular and well formed society, embracing, in one universal bond of brotherhood, all mankind, without any distinction arising from birth, country, education, climate, and colour, who have been admitted to a participation of its sublime mysteries, on the broad principle, that there is no respect of persons in the eye of that all-wise and all-powerful being who created and governs the Universe ; who is distinguished by the attributes of wisdom and loving kindness, and a disposition to do every thing for the general benefit of his creatures. Hence, wherever a mason may stray—even though it be into countries diversified by every variety of manners and customs, language and religion, he will always find a home ;—he will always meet with some kind friend and brother, to give him welcome, to greet him with the right hand of fellowship, to promote his interests, and to give him comfort and consolation in his distress.

It may truly be said of the fraternity, as Archbishop Potter predicates respecting the members of the Church, that they are "united not only by the love and affection, by consent of opinion, or similitude of manners, which may happen to the members of other societies ; but they all bear the same relation to the same common head. This it is, whereby regular Societies are distinguished from confused multitudes ; that whereas the latter are only locally united, and when their parts are dispersed, they utterly cease to be ; the former are joined under the same form of government to the same common head, by their alliance to which their several parts, how remote soever in place, do maintain a strict communion with one another. Thus the several persons who live in the same city or kingdom, are united into one civil society. And the Jews, however dispersed, were all united to God and to one another in the same religious society, having all obligated themselves by the same Covenant, to be the people of God. Whence they are called God's peculiar treasure, a kingdom of priests, an holy nation. And being engaged as one and the same person to him, they are called his Spouse, whence God is said to have married them, and to be their husband. In the very same manner Christians being separated from the world, and united to Christ by the New Covenant, are called a chosen generation, a royal priesthood, a holy nation." And Freemasons, however widely dispersed, are united under a mystic tie, as brethren of the same order, obligated on the same Covenant, governed by the same laws, and practising the same ceremonies. The Constitutions of the society are placed on a firm basis, and the Landmarks are not susceptible of alteration, although the laws which do not affect its mechanism may be modified or changed, with the consent of the brethren assembled in Grand Lodge, to meet the demands or requisitions of any improvement in the state of society; in order that Freemasonry may not remain stationary, while other sciences are making rapid strides towards perfection.

There is nothing to be found in the constitution of the order, but what is perfectly consistent with the principles by which it is governed. Thus the ancient Charges provide that " the rulers and governours supreme and subordinate, of the ancient lodge, are to be obeyed in their respective stations by all the brethren, according to the old charges and regulations, with all humility, reverence, love, and alacrity." These rulers, according to an origi-

K

nal law of revived Grand Lodge, were the Grand
Master and his Wardens; and they were repeated
in every private lodge, which in fact is but a
transcript of the Grand Lodge; although, as the
number of masons increasd, other officers called
assistants, were subsequently added. The constitution of a lodge is essentially democratic, because the rulers and governours of the craft, in
the person of the Grand Master, as well as the
Master of every private lodge, are elected annually
by universal suffrage; every brother having a vote
in the latter case, and the Masters, Wardens, and
Past Masters of every private lodge forming a
legitimate delegation to vote in the election of the
Grand Master.

All actual power is vested, during their term of
office, in the Master and his Wardens; but the
former is the responsible officer, and therefore his
duties are carefully guarded by specific laws, and
solemn pledges. Thus the Constitutions provide
that "every Master, when placed in the Chair,
shall solemnly pledge himself to observe all the
old established usages and customs, and to preserve the Landmarks of the order, and most
strictly to enfore them within his own lodge. He
must also take care that the By-Laws of the lodge
be faithfully written; and that books be kept in
which he, or some brother appointed by him as
Secretary, shall enter the names of its members,
and of all persons initiated or admitted therein,
with the dates of their proposal, initiation or ad-

mission, passing, and raising; also their ages, as
nearly as possible, and their titles, professions, or
trades, together with such transactions of the lodge
as are proper to be written. The accounts shall also
be regularly kept, and the fees payable to the Grand
Lodge shall be entered in a separate and distinct
account. The Master is responsible for the correct
insertion of all the above particulars; and is bound
to produce such lists, minutes, and accounts, when
required by any lawful authority."

The Master of a Lodge, however, has still more
onerous duties to discharge. He must be true
and trusty, of good report, and held in high estimation amongst his brethren. He must be well
skilled in our noble science, and a lover of the
craft; exemplary in his conduct, courteous in his
manners, easy of address, but steady and firm in
principle. He has imposed on him as the Pillar
of Wisdom, the charge of instructing the brethren
in masonry;—not merely by repeating certain
formal passages night after night, which are calculated rather to weary than enlighten the mind;
but to adapt his instructions to the capacity of his
hearers, and to see that none depart unimproved
in moral virtue, and a steadfast resolution so to
adorn their masonic profession, that the world
may discern its influence on their outward conduct,
and learn from thence that its precepts have been
firmly planted in the heart. The Master of a
Lodge is by no means a routine office, although it
is frequently considered to be so; and a brother,

who possesses sufficient tact and activity to work the makings, passings, and raising, considers himself to be furnished with every requisite qualification to rule or govern a lodge.

This is a grevious error; and I have witnessed in the course of my experience, many unfortunate consequences result from an imprudent choice of the chief officer of a lodge. If he be inefficient, his inadequacy is soon discovered by the brethren, and disgust or pity is sure to ensue. They forbear to complain, because he is their own choice. They cannot expostulate, because his authority is supreme, and it is their duty to obey. A secret dissatisfaction is therefore indulged, which is the more dangerous from being irremediable. A writer of the last century, speaking on this subject, has the following judicious remark. " When the body languishes under any secret, lurking distemper, it is always restless and uneasy; perpetually shifting its position, though every altered motion gives fresh pain and disquietude; and thus it is with the mind also; which, once deprived of that ease and quiet on which its health and happiness depend, is ever seeking after new objects to divert its anguish, and deceive it into a momentary and false tranquillity."

In this state of things—the Master's incompetency becoming more apparent every lodge night, —the brethren are remiss in their attendance; defections ensue; and a very serious defalcation in the constitution of the lodge soon becomes visible;

and its declension in numbers and respectability is the inevitable result.

The evils arising from the incompetency of the Master of a lodge, are practically illustrated in the degree of Past Master as it is conferred in the United States. Colonel Stone, who appears to have been well informed on the subject, tells us that the chief object of this degree is to exemplify the necessity of government, and to enforce upon the minds of those who are called to govern, the importance of qualifying themselves for the skilful and efficient discharge of their duties. The ceremonies of the degree are extended to great length; but they are such as strongly impress upon the newly elected Master, a sense of his own deficiencies in the matter of government, and the need he has of promptness and energy in preserving the discipline of the society over which he is to preside. The process of conferring the degree —teaching by practical illustrations—is apparently grave, though withal rather amusing. The Colonel here describes the process, which I omit because it is inconsistent with my plan, but he concludes with these observations. " It is unquestionably true, that in the proceedings I have thus attempted to describe, there is often much confusion and not a little merriment; arising solely from the perplexity, and ludicrous conduct, performed with sober gravity, by the candidate. I shall never forget my own embarrassing exploits when called to this trying station. The laugh at

K 5

a man thus circumstanced, may argue want of grace; but the couplet must be finished in extenuation; for to be grave would exceed all power of face. Still there is nothing wicked, or malicious, or riotous in it; although the noise may be misconstrued by those without the lodge, into the wild uproar of revellers. But a single rap, at the proper moment, hushes all into instantaneous silence. Indeed there is no body or society of men on earth—no meeting or assemblage,—under such strict, immediate, and effective control, as a lodge or chapter of masons."

It is easy for a superficial observer to be deceived in a man's true character, until the solidity of his judgment has been tested by experience. Vivacity may be mistaken for wit, and gravity for wisdom. A brother who is stimulated to obtrude himself into the high offices of a lodge prematurely, will seldom be found to possess the requisite ability for executing their duties with credit to himself or benefit to the fraternity. He is too intent on his own personal aggrandisement to care much for the general interests of the community in which he moves. We usually see, as through a glass, darkly; and, when it is too late, we frequently discover that instead of a wise and judicious chief—instead of a wary and prudent ruler, we have committed our interests to the keeping of an idle jester, or an ignorant pretender. In either case, the reputation of the lodge is put in jeopardy, and it will be fortunate if it escapes public reprobation.

The Master ought to possess knowledge, to diversify his instructions ; judgment, to preserve the happy medium between rashness and cowardness ; talent, to address the brethren at length on every emergency ; tact, to conciliate disputes, and reconcile contending brethren ; and presence of mind, to decide correctly on any sudden indiscretion or irregularity which may occur amongst the members of the lodge, that order and good fellowship may be perfect and complete. He should always bear in mind that a strict and unwavering adherence to the laws, on every practicable point, will never produce rebellion, although temporary dissatisfaction may sometimes occur. But it is always short lived. The evils arising out of disorganization in a lodge are usually the effects of an unnecessary interference in trifling matters, which if passed over without notice, would create no sensation, either of pleasure or pain.

The great secret of government is to understand correctly under what circumstances authority ought to be exercised, and where it would be profitably witheld. The Master may be easy in his manners, and courteous in disposition, but he must beware how he permits any kindness of heart to interfere with stringent duties, or to tolerate disobedience to the laws of masonry. It has been said with equal judgment and truth, that " there is no praise so lightly accorded as that of being *a good hearted man at the bottom.* It is often bestowed on men guilty of notorious vices, and utterly devoid of principle. The secret of this strange appropriation of evil lies in the unstinted toleration with which such characters behold the faults of others. A good hearted man at the bottom will give his hand in amity to the living representative of almost any crime or weakness that can disgrace humanity. He will *poor fellow* the desperate gamester; *good fellow* the desperate drunkard; and *fine fellow* the desperate libertine; in return for all which good heartedness, he expects to receive plenary indulgence for all his own irregularities of every description whatever." It will be easily seen that such a good hearted man at the bottom would make but an indifferent Master of a Lodge. Its respectability would soon be compromised under such rule, and its members would dwindle away till none remained. The Pillar of Wisdom must be of a very different character.

The By-laws of a lodge are usually so clear that they can scarcely be misinterpreted; and being in the hands of every brother, they are universally known. When these are adhered to, according to their literal construction, the interference of the Master would be rather injurious than beneficial, and tend to shake the confidence which the members ought always to have in their chief. But while he overlooks trifling and unimportant deviations, it is his bounden duty to enforce the discipline of his lodge by a strict observance of the Landmarks, and by a judicious attention to every rule whose breach might compromise any prominent principle of the order. He must never exercise partiality, or be detected in the slightest bias in favour of individuals ; but when fine or punishment is incurred, he must be firm in his decisions, and prompt in the enforcement of any sentence which may be found necessary to promote the welfare of masonry in general, or his own lodge in particular.

A brother who possesses all these qualifications, will rule and govern his lodge with honour to himself, and satisfaction to the brethren ; it will represent a well regulated and happy family where harmony and brotherly love will prevail amongst the members ; fraternal affection will preside untainted with strife and discord ; the community will endeavour to promote each others welfare, and rejoice in each other's prosperity ; the order will become respectable in the sight of men, and the Master will retire from his government crowned with all the honours the fraternity can bestow.

The character of a good Master may be summed up in a few words. He has been invested with power that he may promote the happiness and prosperity of the lodge. For this purpose he considers that when he undertook the office, his duties were greatly increased ; embracing many points which require his utmost attention and solicitude. He feels that much will depend on his own example ; for how excellent soever the precepts which he enforces may appear, they will lose half their value if they be not borne out and verified by his own practice. This is the mainspring which actuates and gives vitality to the

whole machine. If his power be exercised tyranni-
cally, the brethren will not love him ; if he allow
the reins of government to be too much relaxed,
they will despise him ; if he be irregular and
dissolute in his habits, they will condemn him.
He must be a pattern of correctness to his lodge,
and never allow his authority to be pleaded in
extenuation of any serious delinquencies.

Tremblingly alive to the responsibility which
rests upon him, he consults the By-laws, and determines to regulate his conduct strictly by their
provisions. He allows no innovations to be practised in the ceremonial or mechanism of the order;
no private committees or separate conversation
amongst the brethren, but keeps them rigidly
attentive to the business before them; no jesting
or ludicrous behaviour which may disturb the
serious avocations in which they are engaged ; no
disputes or unbecoming language amongst themselves ; and while, during the moments of relaxa-
tion, he enjoys himself, in common with the rest
of the brethren, with innocent mirth, he carefully
avoids all excess, and never suffers the harmony of
the lodge to be disturbed by any altercations on
the forbidden subjects of religion or politics ; and
before closing the lodge he cautions them in the
language of an ancient Charge, " to consult their
health by not continuing together too late or too
long from home after lodge hours are past; and
by avoiding of gluttony or drunkenness, that their
families be not neglected or injured, and themselves
be disabled from working."

He is regular in his habits both in the lodge and in the world. Punctual to a moment in opening and closing the lodge, as a stimulus to the correct attendance of the brethren; for nothing shows to so much advantage in the Pillar of Wisdom as this exactness with regard to time. In performing the rites of masonry, whether in the initiation of candidates, the delivery of lectures, or other routine business, he exhibits a seriousness of deportment, and earnestness of demeanour, which attract the attention, interest the feelings, and contribute to recommend the beauties of the system, while they inform the understanding and improve the heart.

There is still another point of great moment to the well-being of a lodge, which depends in some measure on the correct judgment of the Master; and that is, the proper choice of candidates for initiation. The good Master will firmly resist the admission of any person whatever whose character does not correspond with the requisitions contained in the ancient Charges. The candidates must be good and true men, free-born, and of mature and discreet age and sound judgment, no bondmen, no women, no immoral or scandalous men, but of good report; for all preferment amongst masons is grounded upon real worth and personal merit only. This is of such paramount importance, that the Grand Lodge has thought proper to issue a penal injunction on the subject; because "great discredit and injury have been brought upon our ancient and honourable fraternity from admitting members and receiving candidates without due notice being given, or enquiry made into their characters and qualifications; and also from the passing and raising of masons without due instructions in the respective degrees; it is therefore determined that, in future, a violation or neglect of any of the laws respecting the proposing of members, or of making, passing, and raising, shall subject the lodge offending to erasure, because no emergency can be allowed as a justification; nor can a dispensation in any case be granted." To prevent, therefore the introduction of improper persons, it is provided by the By-laws of every lodge, that no person can be made a mason in, or admitted a member of a lodge, if, on the ballot, three black balls appear against him. Some lodges wish for no such indulgence, but require the unanimous consent of the members present; some admit one black ball, some two; the By-laws of each lodge must therefore guide them in this respect; but if there be three black balls, such person cannot, on any pretence, be admitted.

If all lodges were conducted on these principles, they would become, in a more perfect manner, the seat of happiness and joy; peace, harmony, and brotherly love, would ever preside at their social meetings; and they would exhibit no imperfect resemblance of that blessed state to which all good and worthy masons aspire, when T G A O T U shall eternally preside over the saints in glory.

CHAP. IX.

THE PILLARS OF STRENGTH AND BEAUTY.

" When the Senior Warden standing in the West,
  Calls us from our LABOURS to partake of rest,
    We unite, whilst he recites
      The duties of a mason.
    On the level meet, on the square we part,
      Repeats each worthy brother ;
    This rule in view, we thus review
      Our friendship for each other.

When the Junior Warden to REFRESHMENT calls us
  And the Sun is at meridian height,
Let us merrily unite most cheerily,
  In social harmony new joys invite.
    One and all, at his call,
      To the feast repairing,
    All around, joys resound,
      Each the pleasure sharing."
                                        WEBB.

" They that have used the office of a Deacon well, purchase
to themselves a good Degree.—ST. PAUL.

THE duty of the Wardens is somewhat more
restricted. As the Master is presumed to be en-
dued with Wisdom to contrive, so the Senior
Warden ought to be in possession of Strength to
support, and the Junior Warden of Beauty to
adorn. And this explains the disposition of the

L

lodge. The Worshipful Master is placed in the East, to represent the Sun at its rising in the morning, that he may open his Lodge, and employ and instruct the brethren in masonry; to whom it is his duty to communicate light: forcibly impressing upon their minds the dignity and high importance of Freemasonry, and zealously admonishing them never to disgrace it. So that when a person is said to be a mason, the world may know that he is one to whom the burdened heart may pour forth its sorrows; to whom the distressed may prefer their suit; whose hand is guided by justice, and whose heart is expanded by benevolence. The Junior Warden is placed in the South, that he may observe the Sun at its due meridian, which is the most beautiful part of the day, to call the men from labour to refreshment, and from refreshment to labour, that pleasure and profit may be the mutual result; while the Senior Warden takes his station in the West, that at the setting of the Sun he may dismiss the men from their labours, to renew their strength by rest, and close his lodge by command of the Worshipful Master, after seeing that every brother has had his due.

The duty of the Senior Warden, like that of the Master, is indicated by his Jewel of office, which is a symbol of equality, and instructs him that the duties of his situation ought to be executed with strict impartiality, and without respect of persons. Regularity of attendance is an essential part of this office, because if the Master should die, or be removed, or be rendered incapable of discharging the duties of his office, the Senior Warden must supply his place until the next election of officers; and even, should the Master necessarily be absent from any single lodge, the Senior Warden must rule the lodge, if no former master be present.

The Junior Warden is also an important officer. The Jewel by which he is distinguished, is an emblem of uprightness, and points out the just and upright conduct which he is bound to pursue, in conjunction with the Master and his brother Warden, in ruling and governing the brethren of the lodge according to the constitutions of the order; and more particularly by a due attention to caution and security in the examination of strange visitors. Lest by his neglect any unqualified person should be enabled to impose upon the lodge, and the brethren be thus innocently led to forfeit their obligation. The Jewels to which reference has been here made, are termed Moveable Jewels, because they hang pendant from the collars of the three chief officers of the lodge, and are transferrable to their successors at proper times and seasons.

The lodges in the early part of the last century were worked by three principal officers only; and the present assistant officers were then unknown. In fact the office of a Deacon does not appear of any great importance in the business of masonry;

and I suspect that it was not introduced till near the expiration of the century. I am not prepared to name the exact date, because I have not convenient access to any Lodge Minute Books which are earlier than the commencement of the present century; but I shall approximate very nearly to it if I state it to be between the years 1785 and 1790. In the primitive lodges the Worshipful Master stood in the East, and *both* the Wardens were placed in the West. This disposition of the chief officers is evident from every copy of the Lectures down to the year 1784; and the old masonic song, which is still used, proclaims the fact.

> In the West see *the Wardens* submissively stand,
> The Master to aid, and obey his command;
> The intent of his signal we perfectly know,
> And we ne'er take offence when he gives us a blow.

A Continental writer of the period says to the same effect. Lorsqu'on se met à table, le Venerable s'assied le premier en haut du côté de l'Orient. Le premier et second Surveillans se placent vis-à-vis le Venerable à l'Occident.

The station in the South was occupied by the Senior Entered Apprentice, and his business was "to obey the instructions of the Master, and to welcome the visiting brethren, after due proof, first had and obtained, that they were masons." This latter duty was transferred to the Junior Warden when he was placed in the South on the appointment of Deacons, as attendants on the two chief officers; and in a copy of the Lectures which were used about the close of the 18th century, the Junior Warden's office, amongst other important matters, is said to include "the examination of visitors." While in the same lectures, the office of the deacons is simply explained to be, the one " to carry messages from the Master to the Senior Warden;" and the other, " to carry messages from the Senior to the Junior Warden, that they may be regularly dispersed round the lodge." The Junior Entered Apprentice was placed in the North "to prevent the intrusion of cowans and eavesdroppers;" and his duty, at the above period was transferred to the Tyler. It will also be remembered that from the revival of masonry in 1717, no lodge was competent to confer more than one degree; and the Entered Apprentice was entitled to vote on all questions, even in the Grand Lodge. The Senior Entered Apprentice was therefore an important personage, and qualified for the office of a Warden; but he could not be elected to the Chair of the Lodge until he had been passed to the degree of a Fellow Craft in Grand Lodge. In some lodges, down to the year 1780, the above two officers were denominated Senior and Junior Stewards.

In 1745, the officers of the lodges on the Continent are thus described. " Every private lodge possesses the power of chusing its Master (Venerable) from its own members, by a plurality of voices. In France, however, this was frequently a life office.

There were also two other principal officers appointed by the Master, and called Wardens (Surveillans.) It was their duty to see that the regulations of the order were observed by the members; to superintend the ceremonies and lectures under the directions of the Master. Each lodge had also a Treasurer to whom were entrusted the funds of the lodge, of which he was obliged to render an account to the brethren in an especial lodge holden for the purpose on the first Sunday in every month. It had also a Secretary to record the deliberations of the lodge, of which he was obliged to make a report periodically to the Grand Secretary. The office of a Deacon is not named.

There is no mention of Deacons in any of the early Constitutions of Masonry; whether edited by Hunter, Senex, and Hooke, (1723); ditto Anderson, (1725, 1738); Cole, 1728, 1751); Watts, (1730); Spratt, (1751); Entick, (1756, 1767); Kearsley, (1769); Dermott, (1756, 1778); or Noorthouck, (1784). In the year 1731, it was declared in Grand lodge, that the Grand Master, his Deputy, and the Wardens, were the only Grand Officers; and in 1768 a fund being raised towards building a Freemason's Hall, each Grand Officer was subjected to an annual payment in proportion to the dignity of his office. Amongst these offices the Deacons are not registered, although the list extends down to the Grand Sword Bearer; nor are they mentioned in it at all.

In the details of the Procession which took

place at the dedication of the above Hall, although
Noorthouck has particularized the situation of
every officer who was present on the occasion,
down to the Tyler, no Deacons occur. It is clear
therefore, that in 1776, Deacons were unknown
as masonic office bearers. Again, in the Edition
of Preston's Illustrations dated 1781, where he
gives directions for the investiture of the several
officers of a lodge in his description of the ceremony of installation, no mention is made of the
Deacons, while we find them introduced into a
subsequent edition of the same work. In the
Masonic Miscellanies of Stephen Jones (1797),
he describes the above ceremony; and also inserts
the order of a procession at funerals, in neither of
which is the office of a Deacon to be found. These
repeated examples cannot fail to prove satisfactorily
that Deacons were not considered necessary in
working the business of a lodge before the very
latter end of the 18th century.

At this period the number of Masons had increased considerably, and some additional officers
appeared to be necessary to assist in the government of the lodges. The office of a Deacon was
therefore instituted; and as there were two Wardens, the same number of Deacons were appointed
as their immediate deputies and assistants, and
the representatives of all absent craftsmen. The
Stewards are now considered as assistants to the
Deacons, and the representatives of all absent
Entered Apprentices. The duties attached to the

office of a Deacon are, "to convey messages, to
obey commands, and to assist at initiations, and in
the general practice of the rites and ceremonies of
the order." The Jewel of their office is a dove, as
an emblem of peace, and characteristic of their
duties; and their badges are two columns, which
are entrusted to them at their investiture; and
when the work of masonry in the lodge is carrying
on, the Senior Deacon's column is raised; and
when the lodge is called from labour to refreshment, that of the Junior Deacon is raised, and
the other lowered. In the old lodges these badges
were called "Truncheons;" and an Inventory of
the furniture belonging to a lodge at Chester,
taken in the year 1761, mentions among other
things, "two Truncheons for the Wardens."

At the present day Deacons are unknown on
the Continent. The Freemason's Lexicon, a German publication, thus names the existing officers
of a lodge. "Every lodge has officers, viz. 1.
W. M.; 2. S. W.; 3. J. W.; 4. Secretary; 5.
Lecturer; 6. Master of the Ceremonies; 7. Two
Stewards; 8. Treasurer. In most lodges there
are, besides these, a Past Master, a Preparer, an
Almoner, a Hospitalier, and a Decorator. Many
of the first officers have their deputies or substi-
tutes; and the first three are of great importance
to a lodge, especially if they have another and a
better motive for accepting office than merely to
wear a decoration. It is their duty to propagate
Wisdom, Strength, and Beauty; and like the Sun

and Moon, to lighten the paths of the brethren;
but they will not be fit to do this, nor to gain the
love and respect of the members, if they are not
endowed with a zeal for the real objects of the
society, and well acquainted with the means of
accomplishing those objects. They should also
diligently strive to obtain a thorough knowledge of
the mental capacities of all the brethren of their
lodge, in order that they may know how, with
greater certainty and security, to instruct and improve them in masonry."

At the conclusion of this chapter, a few words
on the duties of the members may not be unacceptable; and they may be comprised within a
very narrow compass. As we are none of us free
from faults, it is the duty of every brother to bear
with the infirmities, to pardon the errors and to
be kind and considerate towards those with whom
he is so intimately connected. There are few
tempers so depraved, but a sincere endeavour to
please, will excite in their bosoms, a corresponding
sentiment of love and gratitude. We are under
peculiar obligations, and it is equally our duty and
our interest to discharge them faithfully, and to
the letter. Amidst the various dispositions of
mankind, we must not expect to meet with all we
could wish in every brother who is linked with us
in the indissoluble chain of masonry; but if we
resolve to do unto others as we would have them
do unto us, our happiness and mental satisfaction
will usually be amply gratified. Every relative

and social duty is founded on mutual obligations; and where the seeds of love and friendship are not sown; or where that which springs up from them is not cultivated and improved, it will be but " as the grass growing on the housetop, wherewith," as the glorious language of the Psalmist expresses it, " the mower filleth not his hand, neither he that bindeth the sheaves, his bosom."

A kind and courteous behaviour, therefore, to those amongst whom we live, is what I should recommend and enforce as a branch of masonic duty; because if we hope to be happy in our several stations and professions, and amidst all the misfortunes and calamities which are incident to our present state of existence, we must practise the masonic virtues, not only of Faith, Hope, and Charity; but also of Temperance, Fortitude, Prudence, and Justice. And above all we must be humane, charitable, and benevolent; knowing that whatever tends to ensure the felicity of our fellow creatures will be pleasing in the sight of God; and contribute, in its degree, to advance our perfection in this world, and ultimately to exalt us to " a building not made with hands, eternal in the heavens."

CHAP. X.

THE TRACING BOARD OF AN E. A. P.

> Hail, Masonry! to thee we raise
> The song of triumph, and of Praise.
> The Sun which shines supreme on high,
> The Stars that glisten in the sky,
> The Moon that yields her silver light,
> And vivifies the lonely night
> Must by the course of nature fade away,
> And all the Earth alike in time decay;
> But while they last shall Masonry Endure,
> Built on such Pillars solid and secure;
> And at the last triumphantly shall rise
> In brotherly affection to the skies.
>
> MASONIC ODE.

A chapter on this subject may appear superfluous after the copious illustrations of the Tracing Boards which may be found in the Historical Landmarks of Freemasonry, Lect. iv, v, xvi, and xxvi; but in a Book which treats professedly on the Lodge and its workings, a few additional observations may with strict propriety be offered to render it complete;[1] and particularly as our

---

[1] A Pamphlet has been recently published by the Grand Lodges of the United States, called " the Masonic Trestle Board for the use of Lodges and brethren." It embraces the illustrations of the three degrees of Ancient Craft Masonry,

indefatigable Bro. Harris has just published a
new and improved edition of the Tracing Boards,
which does him infinite credit, and cannot fail to be
of essential service to the Masters of Lodges, in
the instruction which is periodically given to the
brethren on the symbolical machinery of the order.

In the Tracing Board before us, the candidate's
progress in masonry bears a great resemblance to
that of the baptized christian on his road to heaven,
according to the system recommended and practised in the earliest ages of christianity. He enters
into Covenant at the Font, which is placed at the
West end of the Church, where, by his sponsors,
he makes profession of his faith, receives the
O B, and becomes entitled to the white robe as a
catechumen, in imitation probably of the Levites
who were selected by king Solomon to carry the
Ark of the Covenant into the Temple at Jerusalem.
The white garment was delivered with a solemn
charge in this form. " Receive the white and
immaculate garment, which thou mayest bring
forth without spot before the tribunal of our Lord
Jesus Christ, that thou mayest have eternal life."
Such is the commencement of his career in the
Church militant; where, if he contend faithfully
to the end, he will attain the Church triumphant
in heaven.

In like manner the candidate for masonry, being

arranged and adapted to the national system of Work or
Lectures, as recommended by the National Convention, and
adopted by all the Grand Lodges in the States.

duly prepared, is introduced into the lodge at the West end, and having made profession of his faith, by the assistance of his guide, he receives the O B; light dawns upon his darkened mind, and he is invested by the officer in the West with a white or lambskin apron, which he is told is more ancient than the Golden Fleece or Roman Eagle, more honourable than the Star and Garter, or any other order under the sun which could be conferred upon him at that time or any other, by king, prince, or potentate, except he be a mason. If his masonic course, thus commenced in order, be conducted with decency, it affords a rational prospect of being closed with decorum, and terminating in the Grand Lodge above.

The catechumen, having been thus introduced into christianity, was then placed in an inferior rank in the church, with a lighted taper in his hand, that he might be instructed in the mysteries of his religion. He is stationed before the altar as an emblem of that glory which is to come; the taper is a symbol of the light of faith wherewith bright and virgin souls go forth to meet the bridegroom.

The candidate for masonry, having been obligated and invested, is placed at the North East angle of the Lodge, near the pedestal or altar of masonry, with the lights burning before him, to receive instruction; and the Tracing Board being spread abroad for that purpose, the W. M. points out in succession the ground, situation, extent,

M

support, and covering of the lodge, all of which are explained in detail. To ensure his serious attention to the business in hand, he is told that the lodge is situated on holy ground, for which assertion three cogent reasons are assigned, either of which would be sufficient to convince him that any kind of levity would be unsuitable to the place, and subject the offender to very severe reprehension.

The form and dimensions of the lodge are first pointed out and explained. It is an oblong square, extending from north to south, from east to west, from the surface to the centre, and from the earth to the heavens. This boundless extent refers to the universality of masonry, and the influence of its principles and laws over every clime and country of the habitable globe. In the language of the Grand Lodge of Hamburgh, " the Freemason is taught by the principles of his Covenant to love a foreign brother whom he has never seen before, and with hand in hand to form the brother—chain without regarding his dress or his profession ; so too, according to our old Landmarks, the Moslem, the Jew, and the Christian, are received with the same affection, and the gate of the masonic temple is open for all alike."

The situation of a lodge is due east and west because all places of divine worship, and regularly constituted lodges are constructed in that direction for three reasons. 1. The sun, which is the glory of the creation, rises in the east and sets in the west. 2. Learning and science originated in the east, and afterwards spread to the western parts of the world. And the third reason refers to the construction of the tabernacle of Moses.

The most prominent objects in the Tracing Board before us, are three great Pillars, in the East, West, and South ; on each of which is placed a dignified masonic character; and all are still represented in every regular lodge throughout the universe. The one in the East is king Solomon, who stands on the pillar of Wisdom, to intimate that without wisdom to contrive, no architectural work can be expected to arrive at a satisfactory conclusion. The monarch who occupies the pillar in the West, is Hiram king of Tyre, an emblem of Strength, because without his prompt assistance in providing materials and men for the Temple at Jerusalem, that magnificent edifice would never have been completed in so perfect a manner as to make it surpass every other building in the world for riches and glory. And without strength to support, no work how gorgeous and massive soever it might be, could expect to be permanent. The third is Hiram Abiff, the chief architect at the erection of the temple. He is placed on the pillar of Beauty, because it was owing to his consummate skill and genius that it attained perfection ; for without beauty to adorn, a building would be deficient in splendour of enrichment and magnificence of display.

It will be seen that these Pillars represent the Doric, the Ionic, and the Corinthian, which are the only three original orders in architecture.

The candidate is then desired to remark that the floor of the lodge is chequered with black and white marble, or mosaic work, the moral signification of which is beautifully illustrated. It may be observed here that the tesselated pavements of the Romans, being worked in a regular and mechanical manner, were called *opus musivum, opera quæad amussim facta sunt.* Hence the Italian *Musaico,* from whence is derived our appellation of Mosaic; but, like most of our other terms of art, through the channel of the French, *Mosaique.* And Dr. Parr says, as we are assured by Roscoe, in his Notes to the Life of Lorenzo de Medici, "the term Musiva was more peculiarly applicable to this kind of work when used in decorating walls and ceilings ; *Lithostrata* and *Tessellata* being the name of the work, when executed on the floor ; but as the process in both cases was the same, we, in common with other writers, have not hesitated to apply the same term to both, Musiva, Musea, or Musia."

The working tools strewed about the floor are then brought under the candidate's notice, and he is told that the square, level, and plumb, although to outward appearance they are nothing more than common instruments of mechanical labour, yet as they are used by Freemasons to express certain moral virtues, they are as highly esteemed as if they were jewels of inestimable value ; and on this account are appropriated to certain officers of the lodge, as indications not only of their official rank, but also of their respective duties.

The following explanation of these characteristic symbols is recommended in the printed Regulations of the Great Masonic National Convention of the United States, holden at Baltimore in Maryland, A.D. 1843. " The Square teaches to regulate our actions by a rule and line, and to harmonize our conduct by the principles of morality and virtue. The Level demonstrates that we are descended from the same stock, partake of the same nature, and share the same hope ; and though distinctions among men are necessary to preserve subordination, yet no eminence of station should make us forget that we are brethren ; for he who is placed on the lowest spoke of fortune's wheel, may be entitled to our regard ; because a time will come, and the wisest knows not how soon, when all distinctions but that of goodness shall cease ; and death, the grand leveller of all human greatness, reduce us to the same state. The Plumb admonishes us to walk uprightly in our several stations, to hold the scale of justice in equal poise, to observe the just medium between intemperance and pleasure, and to make our passions and prejudices coincide with the line of duty."

On the pedestals of the three pillars we find these symbols repeated, with the addition of others, amongst which we observe a sword and staff in saltire, bound together with a rope; all of which are satisfactorily explained to the candidate, although the illustration would be improper here;—and a Key. Now the Key was always esteemed to be an instrument of power and safety; and was formerly used to inaugurate talented individuals into offices of trust. Thus there was a custom among the Jews in the admission of their doctors, that those to whom they gave authority to interpret the scriptures had a key delivered to them with certain ceremonies. The stewards of a royal household in some countries were distinguished by a golden key, as the symbol of their office; and hence the phrase of giving a person a key was equivalent to investing him with power; and in christianity was applied to the ministers as stewards of the mysteries of God. Peter was the first that preached the gospel to the Jews and Gentiles; and was therefore said to have opened the kingdom of heaven to both; whence he is usually depicted with a key in his hand, as a symbol that he had power to admit and to exclude; by declaring the conditions of admission; by the exercise of discipline, and the administration of the sacraments.

Adjoining these we see another group of working tools, which are peculiarly designed for the use of the newly initiated entered apprentice. They consist of a rule 24 inches in length, a gavel, and a chisel, together with a rough block of unwrought stone; and are thus explained. "The 24 inch guage will enable you to measure and ascertain the size and extent of a work, that you may calculate the time and labour it will take. It teaches you a moral lesson that you ought to apportion the 24 hours of the day into 4 parts and devote them to prayer, labour, refreshment, and rest. The gavel is an important instrument, without the use of which no work that requires manual labour can be completed; and it teaches you the uselessness of skill without labour; for though the heart may conceive and the head devise, no design can be executed without due exertion. By the use of the chisel you may make an impression on the hardest substances; and though small in size it is instrumental in the erection of the most magnificent edifices. Thus perseverance is necessary to perfection; and it is by slow degrees that the rude material receives its polish; and that the most indefatigable exertions are necessary to enlighten the mind, ameliorate the manners, and induce a consistent habit of virtue and holiness. The rough stone, which is called on the Continent Pierre Brute, ou chaos, ou illiaste, ou bylé, is an emblem of the mind of man in its most rude and imperfect state, which can only be brought into form by the force of education and moral culture."

In a corresponding situation on the floor we see a stone perfectly squared and polished, hanging by a winch, and suspended from a Lewis, to symbolize the perfect mason in his old age after he has subdued his passions, and obtained a victory over the three great enemies of his christian warfare, the world, the flesh, and the devil. This is an allusion to Rev. iii. 12, where T G A O T U promises " him that overcometh will I make a pillar in the temple of my God, and he shall go no more out ; and I will write upon him the name of my God, and the name of the city of my God, which is new Jerusalem, which cometh down out of heaven from my God ; AND I WILL WRITE UPON HIM MY NEW NAME." Which Pyle thus paraphrases. "As the pillars of a sumptuous temple are both the strength and ornament of it, so shall all who steadily suffer in my Name, and overcome the lusts and temptations of the world, be esteemed worthy to be members of my future church, triumphant and glorious, wherein they shall remain in uninterrupted felicity, as they have been the honor and ornaments of it in the present state of trial."

The Lewis which sustains the weight of this perfect ashlar denotes strength ; and consists of a certain iron instrument, which being dovetailed into the centre of a stone, forms a cramp which enables the operative mason to raise it, how heavy soever it may be, and fix it with the greatest ease on its proper basis. It symbolizes the son of a Master Mason, whose duty is to bear the burden and heat of the day when his aged Parents are incapable of labour ; to supply their wants and render the latter end of their lives cheerful and happy.

Near the centre of the floor and in front of the pedestal lies a square board on which the emblems of a Master are placed, to intimate that it is devoted to the use of the officer whose duty it is "to contrive" the most efficient designs, and to arrange the materials of the work, that it may be brought to a useful and harmonious conclusion. This is called a Tracing Board, and it contains the ground plan of some public building surrounded by a portico, designed in beautiful symmetry and order; and thus becomes a symbol of the great Charter of our Faith and Hope, the Holy Bible, which is the spiritual Tracing Board of T G A O T U, for in that book he hath laid down such a rich series of moral plans and glorious designs, that were we conversant therein and adherent thereto, it would bring us to a building not made with hands eternal in the heavens.

The candidate now arrives in front of the Pedestal, which the French masons denominate an Altar, in the East, as the catechumen in christianity, after he has gone through all the preliminary ceremonies prescribed by the church, is admitted into the Bema, Chancel, or Church triumphant, to partake of the most solemn mysteries of religion. On the front face of the pedestal there is inscribed a circle and central point flanked by two perpendicular parallel lines, which is one of the most glorious symbols of Freemasonry, when clearly understood and properly applied; but the elucidation is too copious for introduction here. [1]

[1] The Author is at present engaged in an investigation of the origin of this sublime symbol, and of the various interpretations

From this point the Board exhibits a clear and intelligible view of the progress and end of the christian system of religion. On the pedestal is the Holy Bible covered with a square and a pair of compasses. These have a peculiar name amongst masons which denotes their power of illuminating the mind with the rays of divine knowledge. The Bible is the ground of our Faith, while the square and compasses united serve to regulate our Practice.

At the foot of the Pedestal, in the place of Wisdom, and imbedded in an effulgence of light, the candidate sees the glorious vision of a Ladder, like that by which Jacob was entranced during his melancholy journey from Beersheba to Pada-naram a distant country in the land of Mesopo-tamia, when, by the advice of his mother, he fled from the wrath of Esau. It is composed of staves or rounds innumerable on which are seen angels ascending and descending.

This has been usually considered as a symbol of divine providence, which superintends all the works of creation, and dispenses grace, mercy, and justice with unerring accuracy amongst the sons of men. The foot of the ladder is placed on the earth to denote the stability of Providence; and its top reaches the heavens to show that the designs of Omnipotence are without limit; the

which have been attached to it at different periods as it passed through the hands of our brethren of the last century; and the result will shortly be placed before the fraternity.

innumerable staves or rounds on which the angels move point out their ceaseless superintendance over human affairs; the angels ascending are ministers of providence going up to the Throne of grace to make their communications and to receive commands; and those descending are charged with commissions to comfort the souls of the just.

The Theological virtues, Faith, Hope and Charity, each with its appropriate symbol, and the former with her foot upon the Holy Bible, occupy the most prominent stations on the ladder, to intimate that the only true road to heaven is through three gates, of which they keep the keys. No one can ascend even the first step without the assistance of Faith; neither can he pass the centre of the ladder unless he be supported by Hope. The summit is under the guardianship of Charity, to show, that although the christian may have passed through the two gates, yet he must possess a still more benignant and efficacious virtue, if he would master the steep ascent, and enter the everlasting lodge above. The mason who is possessed of this latter virtue, may justly be deemed to have attained the summit of his profession; figuratively speaking, an ethereal mansion veiled from mortal eye by the starry firmament; and emblematically depicted in a mason's lodge by seven stars, without which number of regularly initiated brethren, no lodge can be accounted perfect, nor any gentleman be legally admitted into the order.

CHAP. XI.

THE TRACING BOARDS OF A FELLOW CRAFT AND A MASTER MASON.

> " And he with love of sacred wisdom fir'd,
>   The Mighty Prince whose pious hand,
> To the eternal fount of truth and light
>   That holy temple rear'd,
> The pride and wonder of Judea's land—
>   His great and comprehensive mind,
>   A nobler edifice design'd,
> That time and envy should defy—
>   Founded on truth's eternal base,
>   Vast as the ample bounds of space,
> And sacred to fraternal unity."
>
> RODWELL WRIGHT.

THE Tracing Boards of the second degree are two in number. Some little improvement has been made in the first, which otherwise is essentially the same as that which is described in the Historical Landmarks of Masonry, Lect. xvi, to which I again refer, as it will be unnecessary to recapitulate the explanations which have been made in that comprehensive work, because it is in the hands of every zealous mason throughout the universe.

It will be seen that the two great Pillars are omitted, and the figure of a man has been added who appears entering in haste to communicate intelligence to the ancient Junior Warden who guards the foot of the winding staircase, of the great victory over the Ephraimites, together with some indications of the battle, which are seen in the distance; as for instance, the tents of Jeptha, and the sentinels who have been placed to guard the fords of the river Jordan where the Ephraimites, in endeavouring to return into their own country were recognized by their inability to pronounce the password Shibboleth, which the people of Ephraim, who could not articulate the letter *h*, called Sibboleth. This word means *floods of water;* and therefore they were made to utter the request, " Let us pass over the water." And there fell at that time two and forty thousand men ; which was a terrible slaughter for one tribe to make of another; but the Ephraimites appear to have deserved the punishment for their insolence and temerity in reviling their brethren, threatening to destroy the house of Jeptha by fire, and making a hostile invasion of the country for that express purpose.

The reasons for omitting the two Pillars from the first of these Tracing Boards appear to be because the Middle Chamber, with its approaches by the winding staircase being on the right side of the House adjoining the walls of the Temple, these pillars were not visible from thence, being placed at the entrance of the Porch which opened into the Holy Place. The winding staircase closely tiled remains unaltered. It consists of fifteen steps,

which alone might afford a series of useful and
entertaining speculations to complete our progress
along the mystical ascent; for having passed over
the three, five, and seven steps, when from its
summit we look back upon the latter division, the
creation of the universe is naturally suggested to
our minds, which was effected in six equal portions
of time, while the seventh was consecrated to rest
and worship. They also represent the Sephiroth,
or mysterious ladder of the Jews, consisting of
seven steps, crowned by the sacred trinity.

The winding staircase is flanked by ornamented
pilasters, against which are placed the larger
Cherubim of the Temple, supporting the pen-
talpha and the seal of Solomon. Adjoining these,
and fronting the supports of the gallery or lobby
which leads to the Middle Chamber, are two arched
panels, containing the working tools of a Fellow
craft, viz., the square, the level, and the plumb.
The square is used amongst operative masons to
try and adjust all irregular angles of buildings,
and to assist in bringing rude matter into due
form; the level is used to lay lines and prove
horizontals; and the plumb to try and adjust all
uprights while fixing on their proper basis. By
speculative masons these instruments are applied
to the regulation of conduct. The square teaches
morality, the level equality, and the plumb uprightness of life and action. Thus by the moral application of these working tools the Fellow craft
hopes to ascend to the Grand Lodge above.

In the second Tracing Board we are favoured
with a perspective view, looking from between the
Pillars into the Holy Place, with the Sanctum
Sanctorum at the farthest extremity; and the meeting of Solomon and the queen of Sheba with
Hiram King of Tyre; which have been introduced
as figures that an adequate idea may be formed of
the magnitude of the pillars and the dimensions
of the Most Holy Place. As the name of the
queen of Sheba has been connected with Freemasonry from the earliest times, it may not be
uninteresting to ascertain who she was. Bruce
says that amongst the Arabs her name was Belkis;
while the Abyssinians called her Macqueda. Our
Saviour denominates her queen of the South; and
says that she came from the uttermost parts of the
earth to hear the wisdom of Solomon. It is un-
certain whether she were a Jewess or a Pagan;
but it is clear that she visited Solomon with the
intention of puzzling him by hard and unanswer-
able questions. She appears to have been a person
of learning; because the reason she assigned for
coming to him was to try whether fame had not
exaggerated the report of his wisdom.

In this subsidiary Tracing Board we find the
decorations of the Pillars accurately pourtayed
with lily work, net work, and pomegranates, de-
noting unity, peace, and plenty. Their construction was the first important work performed by
the chief architect Hiram Abiff. Together they
were 35 cubits in height or 17½ cubits each.

Jeremiah says, their thickness was four fingers breadth, for they were hollow and formed of cast brass. The circumference was 12 cubits, and the diameter 4; and the chapiters in all 5 cubits high. They were surmounted by spherical bodies on which were delineated maps of the terrestrial and celestial globes; instructions in which anciently formed one chief employment of a Fellow craft's Lodge. The hollow space within the cylinders was used as archives of masonry and to hold the constitutional records, for which they were sufficiently capacious.

These pillars are surmounted by the acknowledged symbol of the Holy Spirit of God, a hovering dove between two cherubims in the act of worship. The holy place is gorgeously enriched with cherubims, to represent the hosts of angels attending to execute the divine will and pleasure; and also with palm trees and wreaths of flowers. Dr. Kitto justly suspects that these palm trees formed a sort of pilasters; for certainly that seems to be the form in which a palm tree, carved in relief, might be exhibited to most advantage. The figure of the palm tree was well suited for this purpose, or for pillars, or for any form of ornamental exhibition. The selection of this form corresponded with one of the most pure characteristics of Egyptian taste; as did also the form of the lotus, which was given to the only two pillars, of which we read in the description of the Temple. We do not wish to say that Egypt furnished the models which were followed at Jerusalem. We are more interested in observing, that the earliest *written* account of a magnificent building concurs with the most ancient structures that still exist, in testifying that the most ancient ornaments of architecture were immediately derived from the types which nature offered; viz. the lotus or lily, and the pomegranate.

The Holy Place is lighted by ten candles, five on each side, with the altar of incense in the centre. At the west end the Holy of Holies appears through a slight partition between the two curtains which are made to constitute the veil of the temple. Now the tabernacle of Moses had two veils; the exterior one was placed at the entrance of the Holy Place, which Solomon superseded by the erection of the Porch; and the other was the real veil of the temple which excluded the Sanctum Sanctorum from public view. This was rent at the crucifixion of Christ, to show that the most secret mysteries of religion were now unveiled, and the scheme of salvation fully laid open to Jew and Gentile alike, when Christ pronounced the potent words—" It is finished."

Tracing Board of the Third Degree.

On a view of this Tracing Board we are struck with awe and veneration. The emblems of mortality and the resurrection are calculated to extort from us that holy exclamation of Grand Master David, " Lord so teach us to number our days, that we may apply our hearts unto wisdom." In this document the veil of separation between Jew and Gentile is wholly withdrawn, and the mysterious contents of the Most Holy Place displayed to public view. These were the Ark of the Covenant with the Propitiatory or Mercy Seat, overshadowed by the divine Shekinah, which some think was nothing more than the Sacred Name or Word. Landseer conjectures that the Asherim of the Hebrews were surrounded by the Name of the Lord Jehovah expressed in Hebrew characters. This he denominates a Mystery; and adds, "let the reader refer to those passages in the Lamentations of the Hebrew poets where the phrase, *the Name of the Lord* occurs, and let him observe the mingled sentiment of woe and detestation that is felt by the author of some of the psalms, when the Babylonian invaders had violated the sanctuary, and cast the NAME of the Lord to the ground."

The Cherubim, according to the opinion of the Rabbi Solomon, were pictured in human shape, in the form of young men; because the angels appeared in that form to Abraham, Lot, and others; and they were made with wings, because when the angels were despatched on any divine commission, they were said to fly. The description of those which Solomon made states that they stood upright upon their feet; and were intended to represent the glory of God. Dr. Willet, in his Hexapla, institutes a curious comparison between the Cherubim of Moses and those added by Solomon. He says " they differed in the matter, one being

all of gold, and the other of olive tree overlaid
with gold. They differed also in magnitude.
Their wings were spread all one way, and they
stood together; with one wing they touched one
another, and with the other they touched the
walls on each side ; while the Cherubims of
Moses stood at the two ends of the Mercy Seat.
Solomon's Cherubims looked both towards the
east, while those of Moses looked north and south.
In the Holy of Holies of the tabernacle there
were only two cherubims, while in the temple
there were four."

The emblems of mortality which decorate the
coffin, are thus commented on in the masonic funeral
service. " What are all the externals of majesty,
the pride of wealth, or charms of beauty, when
nature claims her just debt ? Let us support with
propriety the character of our profession, advert
to the nature of our solemn engagements, and
supplicate the divine grace to enable us to pursue
with unwearied assiduity the sacred tenets of our
order. Thus shall we secure the favour of that
eternal being whose goodness and power can know
no bound ; and prosecute our journey without
dread or apprehension, to a far distant country
whence no traveller returns. By the light of the
divine countenance we shall pass without trembling
through those gloomy mountains when all things
are forgotten, and at that great and tremendous
day, when arraigned at the bar of divine justice,
judgment shall be pronounced in our favour, we

shall receive the reward of our virtue, by acquiring the possession of an immortal inheritance, where joy flows in one continued stream, and no mound can check its course."

Amongst the most remarkable symbols on this Tracing Board, that of the central cavity where the lost was found, is most conspicuous. By this emblem we represent the beginning of life, and the circle we run until the moment when we arrive at the end, and at our eternal destination. The working tools of a Master Mason consist of a pair of compasses, a skirret, and a pencil. The skirret acting on a centre pin, is used to mark out the ground of a new building; with the pencil the Master draws his plans for the direction of the workmen; and by the use of the compasses he ascertains their limits and proportions with accuracy and truth. These tools, as in both the former cases, are made subservient to the purposes of morality. Thus as the skirret has a chalked line attached to it, it points out the straight line of duty chalked out in the sacred Word of God; the pencil teaches that our words and actions are recorded in the book of God's remembrance to be brought against us at the day of judgment. The compasses are an emblem of divine justice, which has given us a law, and left us free to chuse or refuse whether we will obey it or not, with the certainty of reward or punishment according to our works. If we attend to the teaching of these working tools, and perform the duties which they prescribe, we may live in hopes, through the merits of the Almighty Architect of the Universe, of ascending to the Grand Lodge above, where peace, order, and harmony eternally preside.

The ornaments of a Master Mason's lodge depicted on the Tracing Board, are the porch, the dormer, and the stone pavement. The porch is the Entrance to the Holy of Holies; the dormer is the window which gives light to the same; and the stone pavement is for the high priest to walk on; and his office is to burn incense to the honour and glory of the Most High, and fervently to pray for the continuance of prosperity and peace.

In the open air, above the coffin, a sprig or branch of a tree is depicted, in conformity with the custom of ancient times, when the people of all nations entertained a sacred feeling on the subject of decking the graves of their honoured dead with plants and flowers. It was used to a great extent in this country a century ago, and the disuse of so beautiful a custom is much to be regretted. In the East the graves of deceased persons are still planted with odoriferous herbs and flowers, which are tended weekly by the female members of their respective families.

For a more copious explanation of the symbols before us, I must refer my brethren to the Historical Landmarks of Masonry, vol. ii. Lect. xxvi; recommending them to reflect seriously on the uncertainty of their lives, which may be cut off at a moment's notice; and never to forget that this life will be followed by another which will never have an end. The Tracing Board points out the resurrection of the dead, and a future state of rewards and punishments, to be distributed according to the measure of our faith and practice; and its silent emblems eloquently exhort us so to pass through things temporal, that we may not finally lose the things that are eternal. If we live righteously, the way to heaven is open to us. If we wipe away the tears from the orphan's cheek, and bring him up to virtue and to God ;—if we make the widow's heart to sing for joy ;—if we cheer our worthy, aged, and infirm Brother in his downward passage to the grave, we shall have cause to rejoice in the testimony of our conscience, that in all simplicity and godly sincerity we have had our conversation in the world.

These are the proper pursuits of Speculative Masonry; and if it be practised with a view of increasing the Faith, and Hope, and Charity of its professors; and of producing a luxuriant harvest of Temperance, Fortitude, Prudence, and Justice, Brotherly Love, Relief, and Truth, it will show forth its good works to the glory of our Father which is in heaven. And then

> At thy shrine, O Masonry,
> Shall admiring nations bend ;
> In future times thy sons shall see
> Thy fame from pole to pole extend.
> To worlds unknown thy heav'n-born light dispense,
> And systems own thy sacred influence.

CHAP. XII.

LABOUR AND REFRESHMENT.

> "Aftyr mete they went to play,
> Alle the folk as I you say,
> Some to chambre and some to bowere,
> And some to the hie towre,
> And some in the halle stode."
>
> METRICAL ROMANCE.

"Alexander subdued the world, Cesar his enemies, Hercules monsters, but he that overcomes himself is the true valiant captain."—HOWELL.

OUR brethren of the last century, with a view to the more complete accommodation of the members, had their lodges furnished with a long table extending from east to west down the centre of the room; and in cases where the lodge was numerous, two, flanked by benches with backs—leaving a commodious passage at each end for uses which every brother is acquainted with; and in the latter case, the Senior Warden occupied the north-west, and the Junior Warden the south-west end. On these tables were disposed a pair of 18-in. globes; the perfect ashlar suspended from a Lewis, and affixed to a winch; and sometimes an air pump,

an armillary sphere, and a small philosophical
apparatus, as well as the usual ornaments, furniture, and jewels. The effect was imposing; and
I think we have gained nothing by its sacrifice. I
confess I prefer this disposition of a lodge for
many reasons. It prevents that indiscriminate
arrangement of the members which occasionally
creates much confusion, by placing the brethren
more completely under the Master's eye, and consequently under his command; for in the present
arrangement of the lodge room, opportunities
are afforded for private conventions and conver-
sations, which are the bane of societies constituted
on the plan of masonry, and a violation of the
ancient charges of the order, which positively for-
bid them "to hold private committees or separate
conversation, without leave from the Master; not
to talk of any thing impertinently or unseemly,
nor interrupt the Master or Wardens, or any
brother speaking to the Master." Such conduct
is sure to prove an obstacle to the good government of the lodge, on which the stability and
success of the institution in a great measure depend.

Besides, the table was a genuine Floor Cloth,
or great Tracing Board, not merely affording an
opportunity for every brother to reflect on the use
and application of the various symbols which he
has continually before his eyes, that point the way
to a series of invaluable conclusions, each of which
enforces some virtue, or inculcates some moral

truth that may be brought into beneficial practice during his commerce with the world; but also giving an increased facility of reference to the Worshipful Master in the chair ; and making a more permanent impression on the mind of a newly initiated candidate, by a sight of the symbols brought visibly under his notice, than by merely naming them with the customary explanations. Nothing fixes an object so firmly in the recollection as to have it displayed before the eye ; and therefore it was the laudable custom of some worthy Masters of that period, to point out with a wand to the Rough Stone in the north-east angle of the lodge, the various emblems disposed before him on the table, which were thus more appropriately illustrated, and more readily comprehended. The wisdom which was imparted by this simple process would be esteemed of greater value, because the candidate plainly saw that it was practical ; and the explanations would have more weight, because they would be understood to be reasonable and just; and he would depart more perfectly satisfied that the institution into which he had just been admitted was worthy of commendation and approval.

The removal of the Tables at the Union in 1813, was intended to supersede the custom of taking refreshment during lodge hours, for which they afforded the requisite convenience ; as if moderate refreshment were inconsistent with the solemn business of the lodge. The author of our being

o

has better understood the nature of man. He has
assigned hours for labour and hours for refreshment; and he has appointed certain physical
appearances to determine beyond the possibility
of mistake, the recurrence of those stated periods
of time. The Sun rises in the East, and calls him
to labour; it gains its meridian in the South, and
summons him to refreshment; and it sets at length
in the West, to remind him that repose is necessary
to restore his exhausted strength for another day
of toil. On this principle Freemasonry was originally founded; and no squeamish taste, or fastid-
ious opinion ought to induce us to abandon it.
The practice has received the sanction of all
antiquity, and forms one of the unchangeable
landmarks of the order.

Besides, its disuse precludes the duty of one of
the three Pillars of the lodge, the Pillar of Beauty,
and virtually annuls his office; and how can a
lodge be supported if one of its main Pillars be
removed? This officer proclaims aloud at the
opening of every lodge, that his duty is " to call
the men from labour to refreshment, and from
refreshment to labour, that pleasure and profit
may be the mutual result;"—but in practice he
never discharges any such duty, and therefore
becomes liable to the imputation of negligence,
and his office of inutility. How does this agree
with the ancient charge which directs the Wardens
to be true to the Master and Fellows, taking care of
all things both within and without the lodge, that

the Lord's work be not retarded ? But the Junior
Warden, by our present customs has no option
but to neglect his duty, by which therefore the
Lord's work is retarded, and he becomes amenable
to the penalty of disobedience.

I am not ashamed to acknowledge that I like
the good old custom of moderate refreshment
during lodge hours, because, under proper restric-
tions, I am persuaded that it is consonant with
ancient usage. The following are the routine ceremonies which were used on such occasions by our
brethren of the last century. At a certain hour
of the evening, and by certain ceremonies, the
lodge was called from labour to refreshment ; when
the brethren " enjoyed themselves with decent
merriment," and the song, and the toast, prevailed
for a brief period. The songs were usually on
masonic subjects, as printed in the old Books of
Constitutions, and other works; and although the
poetry is sometimes not of the choicest kind, yet
several of them may class amongst the best compo-
sitions of the day. Each song had its appropriate
toast ; and thus the brethren were furnished with
the materials for passing a social hour. And I can
say from experience, that the time of refreshment
in a masonic lodge, as it was conducted up to the
Union in 1813, was a period of unalloyed happiness and rational enjoyment. All was peace,
harmony, and brotherly love. The song appeared
to have more zest than in a private company ; the
toast thrilled more vividly upon the recollection;

and the small modicum of punch with which it
was honoured, retained a higher flavour than the
same potation, if produced at a private board.
With what a profound expression of pleasure have
I often seen this characteristic toast received :—

> To him that all things understood,
> To him that found the stone and wood,
> To him that hapless lost his blood,
>   In doing of his duty.
> To that blest age, and that blest morn,
> Whereon those three great men were born,
> Our noble science to adorn,
>   With Wisdom, Strength, and Beauty.

Alas! most of the brethren of the times I speak
of, have gone to their long home ; and all but myself have bid adieu to masonry for ever!

During these happy moments, the brethren
entered with much unction upon their refreshments; which were generally conducted with great
decorum in obedience to the old Gothic Constitutions, which direct the brethren to " enjoy themselves with innocent mirth, treating one another
according to ability, but avoiding all excess; not
forcing any brother to eat or drink beyond his own
inclination, according to the old Regulation of
King Ahashuerus; nor hindering him from going
home when he pleases, lest the blame of their excess be unjustly thrown upon the fraternity. No
private piques, no quarrels about nations, families,
religions, or politics, must be brought within the
door of the lodge; for as masons, we are of the
oldest Catholic Religion, and of all nations upon

the Square, Level, and Plumb; and like our pre-
decessors in all ages, we are resolved against
political disputes, as contrary to the peace and
welfare of the lodge." Occasionally, it is admitted,
the masons might and did transgress after the
lodge was closed;[1] for, in the language of a writer
in Blackwood's Magazine,[2] "what says the poet, in
one of those inspired strains by which the gifted
sons of song, flinging the touch of genius around
them, and therewith illuminating and revealing the
sudden mysteries of nature, occasionally announce
sublime truths to the world?

> Punch cures the gout, the colic and the phthisic,
> And is of all things the very best of physic.

Now although this is a poetical exaggeration,
yet it is to be presumed that the most captious
teetotaller will scarcely find any thing reprehensible, amongst those who do not embrace his opinions, if they should imbibe, in the course of an
evening, so much as two or three glasses not much

[1] I find in a printed Letter, dated "9th Nov. in the vulgar
year of masonry, 5738," the following passage on the above
subject. "Some complain that the masons continue too long
in the lodge, spending their money to the hurt of their families,
and come home too late, nay sometimes intoxicated with liquor!
But they have no occasion to drink much in lodge hours; and
when the lodge is closed (always in good time) any brother
may go home when he pleases; so that if any stay longer and
get intoxicated, it is at their own cost, not as masons, but as
other imprudent men may do, for which the fraternity is not
accountable; and the expence of a lodge is not so great as that
of many a private club."

[2] Vol. xlviii. p. 216.

larger than a tailor's thimble. And it is a well
attested fact, that the Freemason's Lodges, even
in those times of universal ebriety, were less liable
to exception than any other associations of the time,
notwithstanding the authority of Hogarth's libel-
lous portrait of Sir Thomas de Veill, in his picture
of Night, which is a wretched and defamatory
caricature, unworthy of its author, although in
keeping with the current slanders circulated to the
prejudice of the craft; for a striking excellence of
the masonic system is, its dissuasives from intemperance; on which, as we have just seen, the ancient
charges are very pointed. Indeed Temperance, as
one of the cardinal virtues, is held in the highest
estimation, in the system of masonry.

When I was the Worshipful Master of a lodge,
the refreshments were abstemious and moderate.
The amount for each brother was strictly limited
to three small glasses of punch, and this was
seldom exceeded, except at the annual festival,
when a pint of wine was allowed; and I am appre-
hensive that a similar regulation was adopted by
most other lodges; at least I never met with an
exception on ordinary occasions. Under such re-
strictions, masonry was not likely to be charged
with intemperance and excess. It is not to be
denied but there were some brethren who displayed
an anxiety to have the allowance increased; but
the character of masonry prevented them from
persisting in their demands; and I should think
an instance of a lodge, in these days, addicted to

intemperánce was not to be found. It would have been a rara avis in terris, nigroque simillima cygno. The mason of the last century, I am afraid, was not constitutionally temperate; but the fault was not in the system, it was in the temper of the times. No public literary or scientific pursuit was carried on without being washed down by numerous potations; and it is sooth to say that most of the private students of the time were addicted to the same practice.

The present age has reversed the custom, and fallen into an extreme equally reprehensible, and at variance with scripture and reason. The principle is carried to such an extent by some of the Grand Lodges in the United States of America, that they have enjoined total abstinence on the brethren as a matter of duty. In the annual Report of the Committee of Foreign Correspondence, appointed by the Grand lodge of New York, in in the year 1842, we find the following passage :—
" Let us commend and congratulate our beloved brethren of Ohio, for having grappled with and subdued a more formidable enemy than even that of rebellion—INTEMPERANCE. The attention of the Grand lodge of this state was directed to this enormous evil many years ago. In June, 1816, the following Resolution was adopted, and is still one of the Regulations of this Grand Lodge.—
' The use of distilled spirits in Lodge Rooms, at the meetings of the Lodges, is of evil example, and may be productive of pernicious effects, and

the same is therefore expressly forbidden under any pretence whatever.' To the fraternity in Ohio, we are indebted for the first bold stand in a subordinate lodge in favour of total abstinence from intoxicating drinks; and while it appears to be universally approved, they condemn any innovation upon the ancient Landmarks; referring the cause to the great and all powerful test of the sublime principles of our order, which disqualify the inebriate from a participation in our rites, and by enforcing which, intemperance must soon skulk from our borders, and be a name known only to be abhorred by every member of the fraternity. Let none be initiated who have the least bias towards intemperance, and let the initiated who are its victims, be admonished, and we shall soon be clear of this blot upon our escutcheon."

We are unable however to give this regulation a decided approval, without first knowing the circumstances under which the injunction has been issued. It appears more reasonable to believe that total abstinence is contrary to our nature, and at variance with the divine intention in placing man on earth.

It is contrary to the nature of man to drink water only, because, in most cases, the element is impure and pernicious. Professor Clark, in his lecture in the theatre of the Royal Polytechnic Institution, on the subject of the impurities existing in water, stated that "serious fears ought to be entertained of the consequences of swallowing the myriads of animalculæ of the most disgusting forms, and of horribly voracious and nimble habits, which abound in what is called the pure beverage of the stream." And he further stated that " notwithstanding all the purification, by filtration and otherwise, of the forty millions of gallons of water which are daily supplied to the inhabitants of the Metropolis, there were still held in solution, in an invisible form, no less than about twenty-four tons of carbonate of lime; or in other words, of that perilous stuff which constitutes the basis of the calculi that, under the various terms of chalk formations, concretions, &c., torment the human frame, and bring it to premature decay."

The bishop of Norwich, speaking of the professors of total abstinence, says, " they are temperate, certainly, but it is a physical kind of temperance. Temperance does not consist in mere abstinence from wine or from spirits, but in abstinence also from anything that conduces to unhinge the mind, and to unfit it for the society in which it moves. This is too much to be seen in teetotalists; they are characterized by a sort of moral intoxication, if we may so call it; when once their passions are excited, they know no bounds; they irritate, oppose, and denounce; which is all foreign to the precepts and principles of the gospel. Again, there are certain fallacies in their arguments which ought to be exposed. They object to anything containing alcohol. Then why do not they object to sugar? Their common sense is at fault as well as their Chymistry. In order to explain the mention of wine in scripture, they try to make out that it is unfermented wine, instead of perceiving that the great principle of scripture is, (as might be illustrated by passages innumerable,) that it is the abuse, not the use of a thing in which the sin lies. I think teetotallers are in some sort, morally intoxicated upon this point; and judging from their conduct upon too many occasions, I might almost say they were labouring under a species of delirium tremens."

This reasoning is consonant with religion. When the Almighty intended to bestow the greatest earthly blessings on his favoured people, he promised to give them for their inheritance, " a land of oil and wine, of fields and vineyards;"[3] because " wine maketh glad the heart of man, and oil giveth him a cheerful countenance."[4] And even under the present comparative neglect of the vine in Palestine, it is allowed that grapes and clusters of most extraordinary size are common. Doubdan, in traversing the country about Bethlehem, found a most delightful valley planted with vines, which appeared to him of the choicest kind. He was not there in proper time to make any observations on the size of the clusters; but he was assured by the monks, that they still found some, even in the present neglected state of the country, weighing

[3] See Numb. xvi. 14.   Deut. vi. ii. vii. 13. xi. 14. xii. 17. xiv. 23. xxviii. 51.   1 Chron. ix. 29, et passim.
[4] Ps. civ. 15.

ten or twelve pounds. Reland also says that a
merchant who had resided several years at Ramah
in this neighbourhood, assured him that he had
there seen bunches of grapes weighing ten pounds
each. Forster mentions that he knew a monk who
had spent eight years in Palestine, and had been
at Hebron in the same district, where he saw
clusters as large as two men could conveniently
carry.[5]

Can the advocates of total abstinence suppose
that all the abundance of rich fruit which Palestine
produced was consumed in its crude state? Do
they forget the wine presses which were subjected
to tithe from their great value?[6] Do they forget
the wine fats mentioned by Isaiah,[7] or the wine
cellars of David?[8] Do they forget that when the
Israelites were threatened with plagues, one of the
severest was, an abstinence from wine,—" thou
shalt plant vineyards, but thou shalt not drink of
the wine, nor gather the grapes, for the worms
shall eat them?"[9] Do they forget that when the
prophet reproved the hypocrisy of the Jews, he
called that hypocrisy a moral drunkenness,—" they
are drunken, but not with wine,"[10]—intimating
that the former was the most debasing vice? They
must have overlooked these, and many other scrip-
tural facts connected with the use of wine, before

[5] See more of this in the Pictorial Bible under Numb. xiii. 23.
[6] Numb. xviii. 27.   [7] Isai. lxiii. 2.
[8] 1 Chron. xxvii. 27.   [9] Deut. xxviii. 39.
[10] Isai. xxix. 9.

they could make up their minds to advocate, under whatever circumstances, the doctrine of total abstinence.

While we contend, however, that the fruits of the earth were vouchsafed by the divine goodness to be *used* by man, let it not be understood that we have the slightest intention of vindicating the abuse of them, which, on the contrary we consider to be a violation of God's gracious design. St. Paul rebukes the Corinthians[11] for being drunken at their feasts; but in the very same chapter, to show them the difference between temperance and total abstinence, he takes wine himself, and celebrates the Lord's Supper. Those, therefore, who would abolish wine because it intoxicates when taken to excess, and would substitute some other beverage of their own invention, even at the holy sacrament, are evidently overlooking the sanction, and violating the command, both of Christ and his Apostles. But St. Paul in his exhortations to temperance, includes meats as well as drinks, total abstinence therefore, to be consistent, should do the same; for in the scriptures, gluttony is always classed with drunkenness, and they are equally condemned.

But while I find the Saviour of mankind recommending " new wine to be put into new bottles ;[12] —when he denominates Judea, which was the finest country upon earth, " the Lord's vineyard " by way of excellence ;[13]—when I find him drinking

[11] 1 Cor. xi.   [12] Matt. ix. 19.   [13] Mark xii. 1.

it himself, and encouraging others to do the same,
by filling six water pots each containing two or
three firkins apiece, with wine, at the conclusion
of a feast " when men had well drunk ;"[14]—when
I see him introducing it as one of the elements of
the most sacred rite of his religion, and declaring
not only that it shall be used to the end of the
world, but that it is also drank in the kingdom
of God,[15] I cannot do otherwise than conclude
that the system of total abstinence is a direct insult
to the Saviour of mankind, by a violation of his
commands, a renunciation of his example, and
setting up our own wisdom in opposition to his
most holy decision.

[14] John ii. 2, 10.   [15] Mark xiv. 25.

Thank you for buying this Cornerstone book!

For over 25 years now, I've tried to provide the Masonic community with quality books on Masonic education, philosophy, and general interest. Your support means everything to us and keeps us afloat. Cornerstone is by no means a large company. We are a small family owned operation that depends on your support.

Please visit our website and have a look at the many books we offer as well as the different categories of books.

If your lodge, Grand Lodge, research lodge, book club, or other body would like to have quality Cornerstone books to sell or distribute, write us. We can give you outstanding books, prices, and service.

Thanks again!

Michael R. Poll
Publisher
Cornerstone Book Publishers
1cornerstonebooks@gmail.com
http://cornerstonepublishers.com

More Masonic Books from Cornerstone

The Three Distinct Knocks
by Samuel Pritchard
6x9 Softcover 100 pages
ISBN 1613421826

Jachin and Boaz
by Samuel Pritchard
6x9 Softcover 92 pages
ISBN 1613421834

An Encyclopedia of Freemasonry
by Albert Mackey
Revised by William J. Hughan and Edward L. Hawkins
Foreword by Michael R. Poll
8.5 x 11, Softcover 2 Volumes 960 pages
ISBN 1613422520

Measured Expectations
The Challenges of Today's Freemasonry
by Michael R. Poll
6×9 Softcover 180 pages
ISBN: 978-1613422946

In His Own (w)Rite
by Michael R. Poll
6×9 Softcover 176 pages
ISBN: 1613421575

Seeking Light
The Esoteric Heart of Freemasonry
by Michael R. Poll
6×9 Softcover 156 pages
ISBN: 1613422571

Cornerstone Book Publishers
www.cornerstonepublishers.com

More Masonic Books from Cornerstone

The Freemasons Key
A Study of Masonic Symbolism
Edited by Michael R. Poll
6 x 9 Softcover 244 pages
ISBN: 1887560971

**The Ancient and Accepted Scottish Rite
in Thirty-Three Degrees**
by Robert B. Folger
Introduction by Michael R. Poll
ISBN: 1934935883

The Bonseigneur Rituals
A Rare Collection of 18th Century New Orleans Ecossais Rituals
Edited by Gerry L. Prinsen
Foreword by Michael R. Poll
8x10 Softcover 2 volumes 574 pages
ISBN 1934935344

A.E. Waite: Words From a Masonic Mystic
Edited by Michael R. Poll
Foreword by Joseph Fort Newton
6 x 9 Softcover 168 pages
ISBN: 1887560734

Freemasons and Rosicrucians - the Enlightened
by Manly P. Hall
Edited by Michael R. Poll
6 x 9 Softcover 152 pages
ISBN: 1887560580

Masonic Words and Phrases
Edited by Michael R. Poll
6 x 9 Softcover 116 pages
ISBN: 1887560114

Cornerstone Book Publishers
www.cornerstonepublishers.com

New Orleans Scottish Rite College

http://www.youtube.com/c/NewOrleansScottishRiteCollege

Clear, Easy to Watch
Scottish Rite and Craft Lodge
Video Education

Made in the USA
Middletown, DE
10 January 2021